Microsoft Azure

Bible

Microsoft Azure

Bible

By

Jason Taylor

2

3

TABLE OF CONTENTS

4

5

Jason Taylor

6

7

8

9

CHAPTER ONE

INTRODUCTION

Welcome to the world of Microsoft Azure! As businesses and organizations increasingly transition to cloud-based solutions, understanding cloud computing has become essential for IT professionals, developers, and decision-makers alike. This book is designed to be your comprehensive guide to Microsoft Azure, one of the leading cloud platforms in the industry today.

Microsoft Azure is more than just a cloud service; it is a robust ecosystem that offers a wide array of tools and services designed to meet the diverse needs of modern enterprises. From hosting websites and storing data to deploying machine learning models and building complex applications, Azure provides the flexibility and scalability that organizations require in today's fast-paced digital landscape.

WHY AZURE?

As you embark on this journey through Azure, it's important to understand why this platform stands out among its competitors. Microsoft Azure boasts a global network of data centers, providing unmatched reliability and performance. Its extensive portfolio of services includes

12

Infrastructure as a Service (IaaS), Platform as a Service (PaaS), and Software as a Service (SaaS), allowing you to choose the right model for your specific requirements. Additionally, Azure's commitment to security, compliance, and continuous innovation makes it an attractive choice for businesses of all sizes.

WHAT YOU WILL LEARN

This book aims to provide you with a thorough understanding of Azure's capabilities, guiding you from the fundamentals to more advanced concepts. We will cover essential topics such as:

- **Core Azure Services**: Gain insights into Azure's compute, storage, and networking options, and learn how to deploy and manage applications in the cloud.
- **Security and Compliance**: Understand how Azure's built-in security features and compliance certifications can protect your data and applications.
- **Development and Deployment**: Explore best practices for developing cloud-native applications, including containerization and serverless computing.
- **Monitoring and Management**: Discover tools for monitoring performance, managing resources, and ensuring the reliability of your applications.

13

HANDS-ON APPROACH

To enrich your learning experience, this book emphasizes a hands-on approach. Each chapter includes practical exercises and real-world examples, allowing you to apply what you learn immediately. By the end of this book, you will have the confidence and skills needed to design, implement, and manage solutions on the Azure platform.

WHO THIS BOOK IS FOR

Whether you are a seasoned IT professional looking to deepen your Azure expertise, a developer eager to build cloud applications, or a business leader seeking to understand how Azure can transform your organization, this book is tailored for you. No prior experience with Azure is required, although a basic understanding of cloud computing concepts will be beneficial.

JOIN THE AZURE REVOLUTION

As we embark on this exploration of Microsoft Azure, I encourage you to embrace the journey ahead. The world of cloud computing is rapidly evolving, and Azure is at the forefront of this transformation. By mastering Azure, you will position yourself as a valuable asset in a technology-driven world, ready to tackle new challenges and capitalize on emerging opportunities.

Let's unlock the potential of Microsoft Azure together and transform the way you think about cloud computing!

AN OVERVIEW OF CLOUD COMPUTING

You are responsible for managing every aspect of an on-premises datacenter, including hardware procurement and installation, virtualization, operating system and application installation, network configuration (including wire running), firewall configuration, and data storage setup. After completing all of that, you are in charge of keeping it maintained for the duration of its existence. This results in high operating costs for the system's upkeep as well as high capital costs for the hardware itself. Even though you can choose the gear and software you want, you still have to pay for it whether you use it or not.

A contemporary substitute for the conventional on-premises datacenter is **cloud computing**. In addition to offering a large range of platform services that you might utilize, a public cloud vendor is entirely in charge of hardware acquisition and upkeep. You turn what would have been a capital expenditure for hardware acquisition into an operating expense by leasing the gear and software services you need on an as-needed basis. Additionally, it enables you to rent access to software and hardware resources that would

15

otherwise be too costly to buy. You only pay for the hardware when you use it, even if you are restricted to the cloud vendor's hardware.

Users can easily manage compute, storage, network, and application resources in cloud environments, which usually offer an online portal experience. For instance, a user can use the portal to establish a virtual machine (VM) configuration that includes the following details: the operating system, any pre-deployed applications, the network configuration, the compute node size (in terms of CPU, RAM, and local disks), and the node location. After that, the user can access the deployed compute node in a matter of minutes by deploying the virtual machine (VM) according to that configuration. Compared to the prior method of delivering a virtual machine (VM), which could take weeks simply for the procurement procedure, this rapid deployment is favorable. There are private and hybrid clouds in addition to the public cloud that was just discussed. Within a private cloud, resources for users within your company. This gives your consumers a public cloud simulation, but you are still solely in charge of buying and maintaining the hardware and software services you supply. By combining public and private clouds, a hybrid cloud enables you to host workloads in the most suitable location. For example, you could host a

16

high-scale website on the public cloud and link it to a highly secure database stored in your private cloud (or on-premises datacenter).

Microsoft provides support for public, private, and hybrid clouds. This book focuses on Microsoft Azure, a public cloud. With the help of the free Windows Azure Pack add-on for Microsoft System Center, you can host a number of the essential Azure services in your own datacenter and provide your users access to a self-service portal. A virtual private network can be used to incorporate these into a hybrid cloud.

A COMPARISON BETWEEN AZURE AND ON-PREMISES

You have total control over the gear and software you use when you have an on-premises infrastructure. In the past, this has resulted in hardware purchase choices that prioritize scaling up—buying a server with additional cores to meet a performance requirement. With Azure, you can deploy solely the hardware provided by Microsoft. As a result, in order to meet a performance need, more computing nodes are deployed in order to scale out. There is currently sufficient evidence that scaling out using commodity hardware is far more cost-effective than scaling up using

17

pricey hardware, even though this has implications for the design of a suitable software architecture.

Azure datacenters have been set up by Microsoft in 19 different locations worldwide, ranging from Singapore to Sao Paulo and Melbourne to Amsterdam. Furthermore, Azure is accessible in two Chinese locations thanks to a partnership between Microsoft and Via21Net. Azure enables businesses of all sizes to easily deploy their services near their clients, wherever they may be in the world, something that only the biggest multinational corporations can do with datacenter deployments. No need to ever leave your office to accomplish that.

Azure enables startups to launch at a very cheap cost and grow quickly as their clientele grows. Creating a new virtual machine (or even multiple new virtual machines) would not require a significant upfront capital commitment. The scale fast, fail fast model of startup growth aligns well with the utilization of cloud computing. Azure gives you the freedom to swiftly create up setups for testing and development. You may script them to spin up a development or test environment, run tests on it, and then spin it back down. As a result, maintenance is essentially nonexistent and costs are kept extremely cheap.

18

The ability to test new software versions without needing to update on-premises hardware is another benefit of Azure.

CLOUD-BASED SOLUTION

SaaS, PaaS, and IaaS are the three general categories into which cloud computing is typically divided. But as the cloud gets older, it becomes harder to distinguish between these.

SOFTWARE AS A SERVICE (SAAS)

Software as a Service (SaaS) is software that is hosted and managed centrally for the final user. Usually, it is built on a multitenant architecture, meaning that every customer uses the same version of the program. To guarantee optimal performance across all locations, it can be expanded out to numerous instances. Usually, SaaS software is licensed via a yearly or monthly subscription.

One of the best examples of a SaaS product is Office 365. A monthly or yearly subscription price entitles users to Storage as a Service (OneDrive), Exchange as a Service (online and/or desktop Outlook), and the remainder of the Microsoft Office Suite (online, desktop, or both). The most recent version is always made available to subscribers. Because the Exchange server is handled for you, including software patches and upgrades, you may effectively have a Microsoft Exchange server without having to buy a server, install it,

19

and maintain it. This is far less expensive and takes a lot less work to maintain than installing and updating Office annually. Dropbox, WordPress, Amazon Kindle, and Microsoft One Drive are other instances of software as a service (SaaS).

PLATFORM AS A SERVICE, OR PAAS

When using PaaS, you set up your application in an environment that the cloud service provider provides for application hosting. The PaaS vendor offers the capability to deploy and run the program, while the developer supplies the application itself. Developers can now concentrate entirely on development since they are no longer responsible for managing the infrastructure.

Azure offers a number of PaaS compute solutions, such as Azure Cloud Services (web and worker roles) and Azure Websites. In either scenario, developers can deploy their application in a variety of ways without being familiar with the technical details. Developers are not required to set up virtual machines (VMs), install the program, and log in to each one using Remote Desktop (RDP). They simply press a button, or something very similar, and Microsoft's tools provision the virtual machines (VMs) before deploying and installing the program on them. Increasing the instance count

20

is usually all that is required to scale up an Azure compute service; Azure then creates new virtual machines and installs the software on them. Azure even manages load balancing on its own. Azure refreshes all of the virtual machines for you when you republish a new version.

INFRASTRUCTURE AS A SERVICE, OR IAAS

You can create virtual machines (VMs) that run on the infrastructure of an IaaS cloud vendor by using virtualization software to run and administer server farms. You can install anything you want on a virtual machine (VM) running Linux or Windows, depending on the vendor. Azure furthermore offers the capability to establish storage, load balancers, virtual networks, and numerous other services that are powered by its architecture. Virtualization software and hardware are out of your control, but you have control over almost everything else. In actuality, you bear full responsibility for it, unlike PaaS.

Because it allows for the "lift and shift" methodology of migration, Azure Virtual Machines, an Azure IaaS solution, is a popular choice when transferring services to Azure. You can move your software to a virtual machine (VM) that is configured similarly to the infrastructure that is currently powering your services in your datacenter. Many programs

21

may be transferred in this way, although you may need to make some adjustments, including changing URLs to different services or storage.

22

CHAPTER TWO

AZURE SERVICES

Azure's cloud computing platform offers a wide range of services. Let's discuss some of them.

- **Calculate services:** This covers Azure Virtual Machines, Azure Websites, Azure Mobile Services, and Microsoft Azure Cloud Services (web and worker roles). Information services This comprises the Redis Cache, Azure SQL Database, and Microsoft Azure Storage (which consists of the Blob, Queue, Table, and Azure Files services).

- **Services for applications:** This includes services like Azure Active Directory, Service Bus for tying together dispersed systems, HDInsight for handling large amounts of data, the Azure Scheduler, and Azure Media Services that can assist you in developing and running your applications. Network services This include Azure capabilities including the Azure Traffic Manager, the Azure Content Delivery Network, and Virtual Networks.

Understanding the various Azure services is beneficial when migrating an application since you may be able to use them

23

to make the process easier and increase the application's resilience.

OVERVIEW OF PORTALS

The simplest approach to manage the resources you deploy into Azure is through an online administration interface. As mentioned in the last section, you may use this to define websites, set up storage accounts, access cloud services, construct virtual networks, and more.

The portal is now available in two versions. The **Azure Management Portal** is the one currently in use. The **Azure Preview Portal** is the new one. You navigate the two portals differently, and they look and feel entirely different. Not every feature—or every component of every feature—has been moved to the Azure Preview Portal as of yet. For instance, the new portal does not currently support virtual networks; scaling an Azure website offers some of the same scaling choices as the previous portal, but not all of them. Some capabilities are only in the new portal, such as enabling and managing the Redis Cache.

The current gateway is a single resource point of view: you can act on a single resource at a time. The Azure Preview Portal allows you to show and manage various resources via a Resource group. In the Preview Portal, you can build a

24

Resource group by identifying a combination of services that work together, such as a website and the database utilized by that website. This allows you to control the life cycle of all associated assets by administering the Resource group. Let's have a look at the two gateways and how you traverse via them.

AZURE PREVIEW PORTAL

The Azure Preview Portal is hosted at portal.microsoft.com. This will most likely appear similar when you first open it.

The buttons for HOME, NOTIFICATIONS, BROWSE, ACTIVE, and BILLING are located along the left side. The Startboard is the area in the middle of the screen that has all of the tiles which contain useful tiles like the billing details for the chosen subscription and the service health. Either right-click the Startboard itself or go to Settings (click your account in the top-right corner) to personalize your Startboard.

Let's discuss the buttons located on the screen's left side. You return to this screen by selecting HOME. NOTIFICATIONS will show the last 24 hours' worth of alerts and notifications. Messages like "Your VM was created successfully" fall under this category.

25

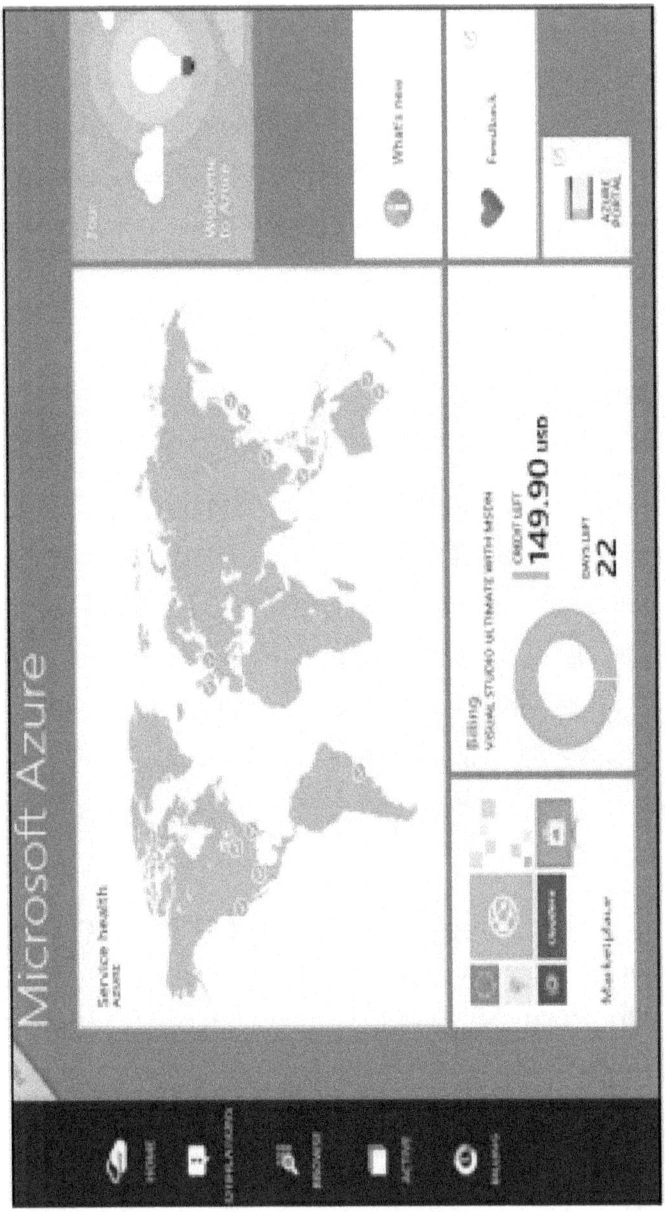
Microsoft Azure
Service health
Billing
VISUAL STUDIO ULTIMATE WITH MSDN
149.90 USD
22
What's new
Marketplace

26

You can filter and jump to certain maintenance-related operations using **Browse**.

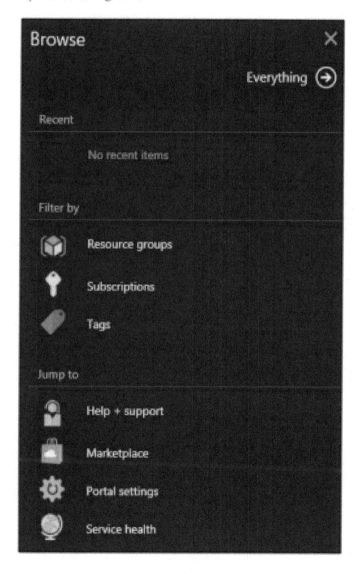

You can filter so that you only see one subscription, for instance, if you manage several. To check how things are doing, you can visit the Service Health homepage or the Portal Settings. Once you begin adding resources to your subscription, the **Browse** blade will display additional items.

You can get to Everything by clicking the arrow in the top-right corner of the screen until then, or if the service you're looking for is not visible. **Active** will show the active journeys that you have open. Journeys is explored in more detail in the next section of this chapter. **Billing** will provide your billing data for the current month.

JOURNEYS AND BLADES

This example's subscription includes a website, a virtual network, and three deployed virtual machines. One of the virtual machines is not on the virtual network, but the other two are. Three virtual machines can be seen if we navigate to Virtual Machines (BROWSE > Everything > Virtual Machines). A blade is the window on the right that shows the virtual machines.

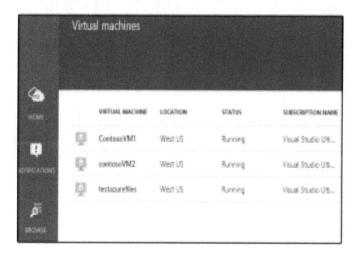

Jason Taylor

The properties for ContosoVM1 are then displayed in another blade that opens when we click ContosoVM1, which scrolls to the right. Clicking Settings on this blade now brings up another blade to the right, where you can navigate to it. We refer to this entire series of choices as a journey. The path we made to the VM Settings is now hidden and will display a blade for virtual networks if we return to the leftmost menu and click BROWSE once more, choosing Virtual Networks this time. If you choose a virtual network, a blade with information about that network will open to the right.

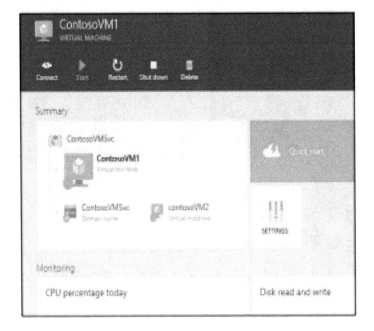

Both of those routes will now be shown when you select
ACTIVE, and you can click either one to return all the way
to the rightmost blade without having to reroute. A window
shows up in the left column when you click the ACTIVE
button. Simply mouse over a journey and click the X that
shows up in the top-right corner of that row to remove it from
the list of active journeys.

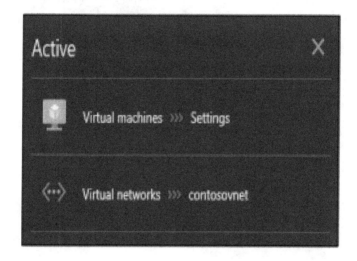

PERSONALIZING THE STARTBOARD

A check box labeled "Add To Startboard" appears when you
create new resources. If you tick this option, a tile that serves
as a shortcut to the new resource will be pinned to the
Startboard. A new tile appears if we build a new virtual
machine (VM) named testazurefiles and request that it be

31

pinned to the Startboard. To set the Startboard in "edit" mode, you can also right-click on it. The possibilities for

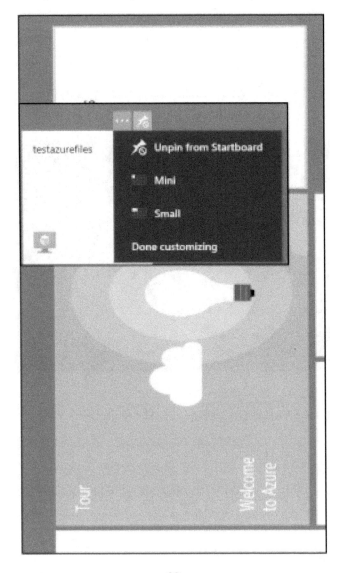

32

changing the new tile. When doing this, exercise caution because you will need to find and re-pin anything you unpin. There's no way to go back.

PORTAL FOR AZURE MANAGEMENT

The Azure Management Portal's live version can be found at manage(dot)windowsazure(dot)com. Let's go to the Azure Preview Portal subscription that was utilized in the example. You can view every resource being used in that subscription after logging in. Every component in the Azure Management Portal is shown. A list of resource categories appears on the left side of the screen. All resource kinds are included in the list that is displayed, which is shortened for space.

You can look at a certain resource type with this list. For instance:

- Click VIRTUAL MACHINES to view your virtual machines.).
- Select ContosoVM1. This launches the virtual machine's dashboard.

33

The DASHBOARD, MONITOR, ENDPOINTS, and CONFIGURE menus are located across the top and are used to navigate the VM's different features. There is a summary for the performance of the VM and different general information such as the DNS NAME available. The dashboard and menu options vary according on the resource type, and the menu options' contents also change according to the resource type. The.NET, PHP, Java, and

34

Python versions found on a website's CONFIGURE screen, for instance, are not applicable to a virtual machine (VM) and are therefore not displayed on the VM's dashboard.

virtual machines

INSTANCES   IMAGES   DISKS

NAME	STATUS	SUBSCRIPTION	LOCATION	DNS NAME
ContosoVM	Running	Visual Studio Ultimate ...	West US	contosovm.com
contosoVM2	Running	Visual Studio Ultimate ...	West US	contosovmvc.clou
testazurefiles	Running	Visual Studio Ultimate ...	West US	testazurefilestest.c

35

There is a context-aware menu, or command bar, across the
bottom. Depending on the resource being used, it varies.

The resource that is shown also affects this menu. At the bottom of the screen, directly above the command bar, are notifications.

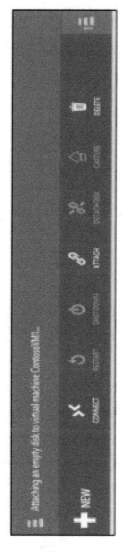

37

BILLING AND SUBSCRIPTION ADMINISTRATION

Azure services can be accessed through a variety of subscription types. To access these subscriptions, you need either a work or school account (provided by an administrator for commercial or academic usage) or a Microsoft account (established by you for personal use). Let's examine the most popular subscriptions:

- **Free trial**: The top page of Azure.com has an option to register for a free trial. This provides you with a You can test out any mix of Azure resources for a month with a $200 credit. Your trial will end if you use more credit than you have. Your services will be terminated and rendered inoperable at the conclusion of the trial. At any point, you can switch to a pay-as-you-go membership.

- **MSDN subscriptions**: An MSDN subscription entitles you to a certain amount in Azure credit every month. For instance, you receive $100 in Azure credit each month if you have a Visual Studio Premium with MSDN subscription. Your service will be suspended until the beginning of the following month if you go over the credit limit. You can add a credit card to be used for the extra expenses and

38

disable the spending cap. MSDN accounts are eligible for a discount on some of these expenses. For instance, you receive a discount of 33% on virtual machines for Windows. Because of this, MSDN accounts are perfect for test and development settings.

Keep in mind that development and testing, not production, are the intended uses for these subscriptions. Access to all of Microsoft's software for development and test environments for up to five MSDN accounts is only one of the many advantages that the BizSpark program offers to entrepreneurs. In addition to these perks, you pay less for a number of Azure services, including Windows Virtual Machines, and receive $150 in Azure credit for each of those five MSDN accounts.

Visit http://azure(dot)microsoft(dot)com/en-us/offers/ms-azr-0064p/ for additional details.

- **Pay-as-you-go**: With this subscription, you link a credit or debit card to the account and only pay for the services you use. You may also be authorized to invoice if you are an organization.
- **Enterprise agreements**: Under an enterprise agreement, you pay in advance and commit to using

39

a specific number of Azure services over the course of the following year. Your commitment gets used up throughout the course of the year. You can pay for the extra consumption on a quarterly or annual basis if you go above the commitment amount. You receive a discount on Azure services based on the size of your commitment.

DISTRIBUTE YOUR AZURE SUBSCRIPTION'S ADMIN RIGHTS

You can grant administrative access to other Microsoft accounts after registering for an Azure subscription using your Microsoft account. Depending on whether you are using the Azure Management Portal or the Azure Preview Portal, there are differences in how this is done. You must grant the new account access to both portals if you want it to have access to both. The reason for this is that the Azure Management Portal does not employ Role-Based Access Control (RBAC), whereas the Azure Preview Portal does. With the help of RBAC, you may give account management more precise permissions than merely complete access to a subscription.

You must add the OWNER role for the subscription to the user's account in order to grant them the ability to change the resources in the subscription through the Azure Preview

40

Portal.

You must add the user's account as a co-administrator to the subscription in order to give them administrative access to their Azure Management Portal account. The user cannot add or remove other co-administrators or change the service administrator with this account, but it will have all the same rights as the original subscription owner.

When requesting access to an account in either portal, the account is automatically added to the subscription's default Azure Active Directory if it isn't already there. The Azure Management Portal allows you to monitor and manage the Active Directory users. In each of the portals, let's examine how we might grant someone access to a subscription.

HOW TO GIVE THE AZURE PREVIEW PORTAL ADMINISTRATOR ACCESS

- Log into your Azure account by visiting the Azure Preview Portal (portal.azure.com).
- On the left side of the screen, click BROWSE. Next, choose Subscriptions.
- There should be at least one subscription visible on the Subscriptions blade that opens. To add an administrator, click on the one you wish to add. The Subscription blade is now open.

41

- To view the list of roles, select the Roles tile in the Access section.

- You must assign the account to the OWNER role in order to add an administrator. To reveal the Owner blade, click OWNER. Subscription administrators is the only user in this account with the Owner role. You can view the role, the group to which it belongs

42

(Subscription admins), and the subscription to which it belongs (in this case, Visual Studio Ultimate with MSDN) by clicking the owner.

- At the top of the Owner blade, click +Add. This brings up the Add Users blade, where you can choose which account you wish to give OWNER access to. You can look for an account by name or email address, or you can choose one from the entries that are shown in the default Active Directory. You will be notified that the account will be added automatically if it is not in the default Active Directory.

- Click Select at the bottom of the blade after selecting the account. You can now see that the account has been assigned to the Owner role once it refreshes the Owner blade. You may manage the subscription by logging in with that account. Currently, this account may administer the Azure Preview Portal, but not the other portal.

In Azure Management Portal:

- Add a co-administrator.

- Go to manage(dot)windowsazure(dot)com, the Azure Management Portal, and log in.

43

- On the left, click SETTINGS.

- To specify the co-administrator, choose ADMINISTRATORS on the SETTINGS screen, and then click ADD+ at the bottom of the screen.

- In the lower-right corner of the screen, click the check box after entering the email address and choosing the subscription you want that individual to be able to manage. It will display the subscription for

44

which the account is now a co-administrator and add this to the ADMINISTRATORS panel.

The Azure Management Portal now allows this account to manage the subscription.

CALCULATOR FOR PRICES

The pricing calculator at http://azure.microsoft.com/en-us/pricing/calculator/ can be used to estimate the cost of your Azure infrastructure. Every Azure service has a distinct price. You can choose a performance level that is suitable for your use of the service because many Azure services provide basic, standard, and premium tiers, each of which typically has multiple price and performance levels. The price estimate appears at the bottom of the page as you make changes. You can use the entire calculator to estimate several features at once, or you can examine each feature independently.

To see the Website cost, for instance, click Websites. Choose a bandwidth value (ingress is free) after clicking Standard and configuring the size and quantity of virtual machines. At the bottom, the price is computed and tallied.

You can choose from options specific to each functionality. For instance, you can specify the following if you choose:

45

- **Virtual Machines**: The kind of virtual machines you desire and the number of each chosen.
- **Windows virtual machines**: D-Series or A-Series, Basic or Standard Linux virtual machine: D-Series or A-Series, Basic or Standard SQL Server virtual machine: Web, Standard, or Enterprise edition; D-Series or A-Series
- **Basic, Standard, or Enterprise editions of Biztalk Server Oracle**: Various Oracle software options, either basic or standard Bandwidth (egress)

If you choose Mobile Services, you can specify the following, which is another instance of the choices being service-dependent:

- Tier: Standard, Basic, and Free

Should a SQL Database Bandwidth (egress) be included? The quantity of push alerts received each month When assessing your Azure expenses, the pricing calculator can be a great resource. Keep in mind that it excludes regional variations, but you can find those by selecting the area on the individual service pricing pages at http://azure(dot)microsoft(dot)com/en-us/pricing/.

46

- **Billing**: The ability to view your billing data is a crucial aspect of using Azure. Knowing how much you have left and seeing where the expenses are mounting are helpful if you have an account, like an MSDN account, that gives you a specific amount of credit. By default, this appears in the Azure Preview Portal's Startboard.

To view this data, you can also select the BILLING option from the menu on the Startboard's left side. More details are available if you click that tile or choose the subscription on the BILLING blade. This displays the remaining credit, the billing period details, and the burn rate—the pace at which expenses are mounting. To help you see where the expenses are, the bottom of that blade displays the charges broken down per Azure service. Clicking on this tile will display the Resource Costs data.

Managing the expenses for your Azure membership is made much easier with the opportunity to regularly view the billing information. You can detect whether you're approaching the cap if your membership has a monthly credit. Additionally, you can see where your expenses are mounting. Additionally, because they will have billing connected with them, you will be able to see virtual

47

machines (VMs) if you provision them and forget they are out there.

CHAPTER THREE
AZURE CLOUD SERVICES AND AZURE WEBSITES

This chapter examines Azure Websites and Azure Cloud Services, two Platform as a Service (PaaS) option in Microsoft Azure. We explain what Azure Websites is, how to build websites with the service, and how to maintain them. We also examine Azure's choices for prebuilt websites. Applications are deployed onto instances (virtual machines [VMs]) of server kinds known as web roles and worker roles using Cloud Services, a PaaS compute capability. Because Microsoft fully manages the instance deployment, scaling apps in and out is simple. This functionality should not be confused with Cloud Services.

BUILDING AND SETTING UP WEBSITES

This section explains Azure Websites, goes over some of its features, and walks you through the process of building, configuring, and scaling websites.

AZURE WEBSITES: WHAT IS IT?

With the help of Azure Websites, a managed cloud service, you can quickly launch a web application and make it accessible to your clients online. The virtual machines (VMs) that power your website are managed for you; you don't provide direct support for them. Supported languages include .NET, Java, PHP, Node.js, and Python. In addition to building your own website, you can start with a number of online apps, including WordPress, Umbraco, Joomla!, and Drupal.

To ensure that a new version of the website is launched each time you commit a change, you can utilize continuous deployment with Team Foundation Server (TFS), Git, or GitHub.

On demand, you can scale the number of instances in and out; alternatively, you can set up autoscaling, which allows Azure to scale it in or out for you according on certain performance metrics like CPU Percentage. You can set up load balancing to maximize your resources if your website has numerous instances. Performance data, application logging, web server logging, and IIS can all be gathered for diagnostic purposes.

IIS Failed Request logs and logs. You can even remotely debug your application while it's running in the cloud if you're using Microsoft Visual Studio. To put it briefly, Azure Websites offers a plethora of tools that facilitate the deployment, management, and troubleshooting of online applications.

50

HOW TO BUILD A NEW WEBSITE

Let's design a fresh website. We will post content to the website later in this part.

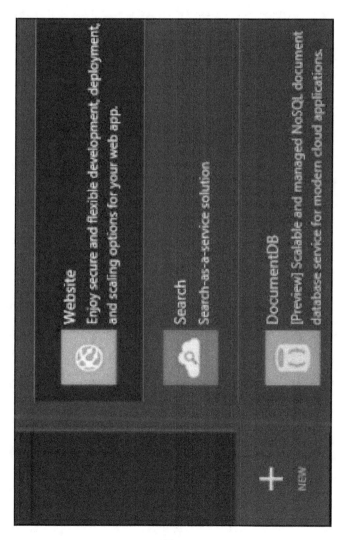

- Log into the Microsoft Azure Preview Portal (portal.azure.com) to get started.
- You now require an Azure account.
- You can register for a free trial at azure.microsoft.com if you don't already have one.
- Making use of the portal, click the large +NEW icon in the bottom-left corner of the screen after logging into the portal, then choose Website.
- Every entry used in Azure Websites must have a unique URL. A green square featuring a smiley face will appear if it is accepted.

Keep in mind that the URL for the website will be created by appending whatever prefix is entered here with.azurewebsites.net.

- The name of the subscription linked to the Microsoft account you used to log in is displayed under SUBSCRIPTION. You can click SUBSCRIPTION and choose the subscription you wish to use if you manage several accounts with a single Microsoft account.
- The area of the datacenter where the website will be hosted is called LOCATION. Choose the location

52

that is nearest to you. Accept the RESOURCE GROUP default.

The WEB HOSTING PLAN establishes how the website's resources—such as memory and core counts, local storage capacity, and available services like backups and autoscaling—are distributed.

- Clicking the WEB HOSTING PLAN option will bring up a panel. After choosing the plan you desire, you may give your new web hosting package a name. That screen does not show all of the plans.

- You can view all of the pricing tiers by selecting the BROWSE ALL PRICING TIERS option that appears when you scroll past what is shown here and below the OK button.

- Or Use Existing, which essentially advises against creating a new web hosting plan, is under that option.

- Choose the free tier or Use Existing if the free tier is your default.

- Click Create at the bottom of the new website screen after selecting the Add To Startboard check box and leaving the other fields set to their default values.

53

As shown, Azure will build your new website, pin it to your portal's Startboard for easy access, and display the website and its properties.

- You may view all of the options by clicking the three dots to the right of SWAP: A new webpage is added by ADD.

- BROWSE launches the browser and displays your webpage. It displays the default page with links to other deployment tools if you haven't published anything yet.

- The webpage is started and stopped using START/STOP.

- Deployment environments are switched by SWAP. For instance, you can publish and test your website to staging if you have both a production and a staging environment. Once you're happy with it, you may use the SWAP option to promote it to production and

55

then delete the staging environment, which is now the previous production version.

- Your website is restarted using RESTART. The website is deleted from your account when you select DELETE.

- RESET PUBLISH PROFILE invalidates the previous credentials and resets the publishing credentials; These are the login credentials for Git and FTP.

- Visual Studio's GET PUBLISH PROFILE function retrieves the data required to publish a website. You can modify the size, instance count, and other aspects of the host that the website is hosted on with the WEB HOSTING PLAN.

- As of right now, you have made a new Azure website, but you haven't added any content to it. We'll take care of that later in this chapter in the section titled "Publishing a website from Visual Studio."

GALLERY OF WEBSITES

Let's examine some of the website possibilities offered by the Azure Marketplace while we examine the Azure Preview Portal. On the left side of the page, click BROWSE. Next, choose Marketplace. To see the website options in the Marketplace blade, choose Web. You can use a number of

56

premade websites and templates that are available here. Scrolling down will reveal the categories.

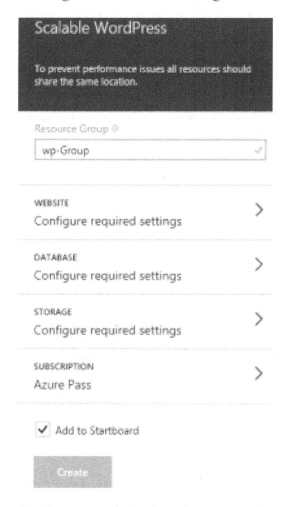

Clicking More at the end of any row will display more possibilities within that category. Some of the options that are shown are as follows: CMSs and blogs: Drupal, Umbraco CMS, Joomla!, DNN, WordPress, and MonoX. Examples of starter sites include ASP.NET, HTML5, Node.js, and PHP, such as a website for a bakery. Choose Scalable WordPress—it displays information on the right-hand side. At the bottom of the window, click Create. This brings up a window that allows you to customize your WordPress website.

A website and a database are two examples of Azure resources that can be seen and managed by grouping them together using the RESOURCE GROUP feature. After doing that, click Configure Required Settings under WEBSITE. The WEB HOSTING PLAN (as previously mentioned), the LOCATION (the area where the datacenter is located), and the WEB APP SETTINGS (which comprise different keys and SALT values) are examples of WEBSITE settings. The DATABASE NAME, pricing tier, datacenter location, and LEGAL TERMS are among the DATABASE options that essentially allow Microsoft to charge you for the MySQL database service.

You can choose an existing storage account or create a new one for the website to utilize in the STORAGE settings. Click CREATE once the setup details have been entered.

Azure will build your WordPress website. As an administrator, you can access it and make any necessary modifications.

HOW TO SET UP AND EXPAND A WEBSITE

Let's examine the Azure Management Portal's (manage(dot)windowsazure(dot)com) website configuration and scalability options. (Not every functionality is yet accessible through the Azure Preview Portal.)

- Click on one of your websites after logging in and choosing WEB SITES from the left column. Setting up
- Click the CONFIGURE option at the top of the page to view the website's configuration settings.
- You have the ability to manage your Secure Sockets Layer (SSL) bindings, upload certificates, and manage domains.

CERTIFICATIONS

An SSL certificate can be uploaded here. End consumers can visit your website over HTTPS if you have linked your SSL certificate to your unique domain name.

59

Jason Taylor

NAMES FOR DOMAINS

This enables you to use a custom domain rather than
mywebsiteatcontoso(dot)azurewebsites(dot)net, such as
mywebsite(dot)contoso(dot)com.

60

SSL CONNECTIONS

This is where the custom domain name and SSL certificate are bound. Oversee the website's SSL bindings, domain names, and certificates. Configuring application diagnostics is done in the following section. All the parameters are turned on to display as much as possible in the picture.

ON/OFF APPLICATION LOGGING (FILE SYSTEM)

Any logging that the web application does will be written to the file system if this is enabled. By FTPing into the website, you can view the logs. Due to the restricted disk capacity, this will be activated for 12 hours before turning off on its own. Error, Warning, Information, and Verbose are among the logging levels.

APP LOGGING (ON/OFF) FOR TABLE STORAGE

Any logging done by the web application will be written to Azure Tables if this is enabled. Error, Warning, Information, and Verbose are among the logging levels. You will be offered to use the storage account and table if you choose this option. There is never an automated deletion of these logs.

BLOB STORAGE (APP LOGGING) (ON/OFF)

If enabled, the logs are written to Azure Blob storage, where they are stored in distinct blobs for each hour. You can set a retention period in days for these logs; if you leave it empty, the logs will never be automatically erased. You will be

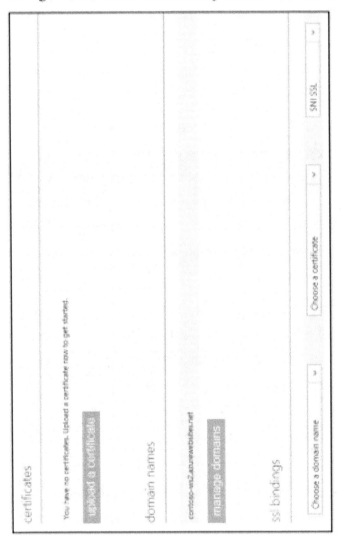

asked for the storage account and container if you choose this option.

Jason Taylor

Manage Table Storage for
Application Diagnostics

STORAGE ACCOUNT

nightbirdstorage ▾

WINDOWS AZURE TABLE

Create a new table ▾

TABLE NAME

wawsapplogtablecontoso-ws2

✓

64

Configuring site diagnostics is done in the following part.

LOGGING INTO THE WEB SERVER (OFF/STORAGE/FILE SYSTEM)

This specifies whether the local file system or Azure Tables should receive the web server (IIS) logs. If you select FILE SYSTEM or STORAGE, you can specify the keeping period. The QUOTA, or maximum disk space that the logs can occupy, can also be adjusted for the FILE SYSTEM and must be between 25 MB and 100 MB.

ERROR MESSAGES IN DETAIL (ON/OFF)

This lets you know if you should produce detailed or summary error messages.

REQUEST TRACING FAILED (ON/OFF)

This shows if the IIS Failure Logs should be written.

site diagnostics

WEB SERVER LOGGING	OFF	STORAGE	FILE SYSTEM

QUOTA	35	MB

SET RETENTION	☑

RETENTION PERIOD	14	days

DETAILED ERROR MESSAGES	ON	OFF

FAILED REQUEST TRACING	ON	OFF

You can set up remote debugging in the following part. You can use Visual Studio to attach a debugger and debug your website while it's running in Azure if you enable this and publish a debug version of your website.

You can designate up to two endpoints to be watched in the following section. By setting this up, you may keep an eye

67

on the availability of HTTP or HTTPS endpoints from up to

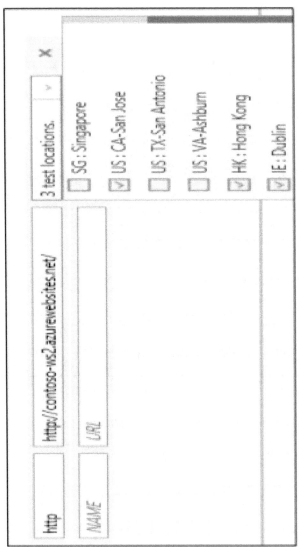

three different locations: Ashburn, Virginia; San Antonio,

Texas; Chicago, Illinois; Amsterdam; Singapore; and Hong Kong. This might assist you in identifying latency globally if your application is used overseas.

Setting up and managing various deployment slots for your website, including staging and production, is the single feature of the Azure Preview Portal that is absent from the Azure Management Portal. This can be found in the Azure Preview Portal's Configuration section (portal.azure.com).

THE SCALING

A free website can only have one instance and cannot be scaled. A basic website can be manually scaled to three instances. You have to utilize a Standard website for autoscaling, which permits up to ten instances. Since not all of the features have been moved to the Azure Preview Portal yet, let's examine the possibilities using the Azure Management Portal (manage.windowsazure.com). We must first confirm if the web hosting package is STANDARD.

- Choose the website you wish to configure or autoscale by logging into the Azure Management Portal (manage(dot)windowsazure(dot)com), clicking WEBSITES in the left column.
- At the top of the screen, select SCALE.

69

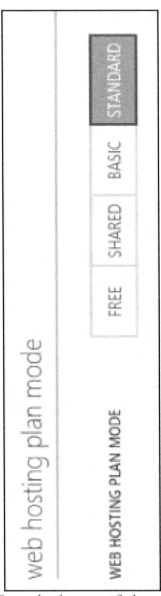

- Click SAVE at the bottom of the screen after

70

selecting STANDARD to modify your plan.

Keep in mind that this screen also allows you to modify the Instance Size, or the total number of instances. Compared to the Azure Management Portal, the Azure Preview Portal contains additional information about the web hosting plan.

- Go to portal(dot)azure(dot)com, choose your website, and then click WEB HOSTING PLAN in the top actions to view those possibilities.
- Make sure to return to the Azure Management Portal to continue if you do that now.
- The scale choices are now displayed as we have a standard website.
- You can start by scaling in accordance with a timetable. When you select Set Up Schedule Times, the entry screen will appear.

71

Set up schedule times

RECURRING SCHEDULES ☀

☐ Different scale settings for day and night ⓘ

☐ Different scale settings for weekdays and weekends ⓘ

TIME

Day starts: 8:00 AM ∨   Day ends: 8:00 PM ∨

Time zone: (UTC-08:00) Pacific Time (US & Canada) ∨

SPECIFIC DATES ⓘ

NAME	START AT	START TIME	END AT	END TIME
NAME	*YYYY-MM-DD*	*HH:MM AM/PM*	*YYYY-MM-DD*	*HH:MM AM/PM*

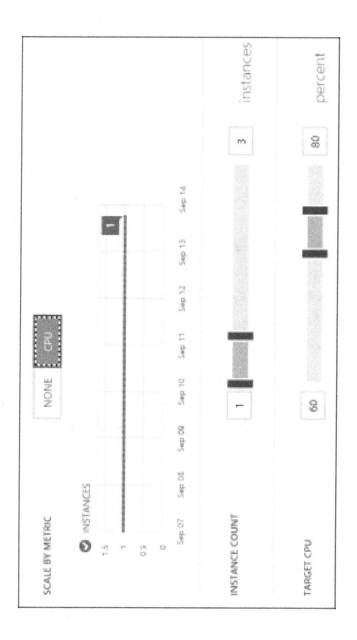

There are a number of choices, as you can see. Setting a default schedule and then overriding it for particular dates is another option. For instance, you might want to override that on a holiday if you're scaling up from 8 a.m. to 5 p.m. Additionally, you can scale by CPU Percentage, as indicated.

The number of occurrences throughout the previous week is displayed in this chart. Before setting the TARGET CPU for the scaling, you can provide the minimum and maximum number of instances (INSTANCE COUNT). In this example, the number of instances will increase to three when the CPU reaches 60% and decrease to one when it falls below 60% once more. Autoscaling with Azure Websites takes roughly five minutes.

SETTING UP AND KEEPING AN EYE ON WEBSITES

This section examines the possibilities for content creation, demonstrates how to publish your website using Visual Studio, and examines the Azure Management Portal's monitoring features.

WEBSITE CREATION OPTIONS

When it comes to building a website and uploading the content to Azure Websites, there are several choices. Notepad or an HTML editor.

74

Although this is a somewhat constrained method of building a website, if you're just starting out with web development and would want to make a basic HTML page, you can use **Notepad** or your preferred editing tool for **HTML**. Once you're finished, you can move the files to the website via FTP.

- Go to the Azure Management Portal, click Websites, and then choose your website to FTP your files to it.
- Click Reset Your Deployment Credentials in the "quick glance" column if you haven't already configured your login information.
- Enter your username and password when asked. This is for FTP or Git access.

The FTP HOST NAME and the DEPLOYMENT / FTP USER are also listed under the "quick glance" column. Together with the password, you will need these two pieces of information to access your website and upload your files when you FTP in.

THE WEBMATRIX

You can design, publish, and manage your websites with this free, lightweight, cloud-connected web development tool. This is available for download at http://www(dot)microsoft(dot)com/web/webmatrix/.

75

Jason Taylor

The following are some of this application's features: smooth connection to Azure Websites. PHP, Node.js, ASP.NET, HTML5, CSS3, and jQuery are all compatible.

This allows you to support a large number of websites found in the Azure Management Portal's Website Gallery or the Azure Preview Portal's Website Marketplace. Umbraco, WordPress, Joomla!, and Drupal are a few of the websites that are available enables MySQL, SQL Server, and SQL CE database administration. integrates easily with TFS and Git. WebDeploy or FTP can be used to create websites locally or remotely.

You can develop a new web application using one of the available templates, publish it, and log in with the Microsoft account you use for Azure. Your new web application will appear when you log into either of the Azure Management Portals. Modifications can be made, the outcomes checked in the local browser, and then republished. Republishing merely makes the updated files available. Visual Studio

Using languages like C#, C++, VB, F#, and XAML, Visual Studio is a comprehensive development environment that enables you to create a wide range of applications, including but not limited to ASP.NET MVC applications, .NET client

76

applications, Windows Communication Foundation (WCF) services, Web API, and Cloud Services. You may develop a new web application using Visual Studio and publish it straight to Azure Websites. In the following part, we'll examine how to accomplish this.

HOW TO UTILIZE VISUAL STUDIO TO PUBLISH A WEBPAGE

In Visual Studio, launch one of your web apps. If you don't already have a web application, use Visual Studio to build one by choosing FILE > NEW PROJECT, choosing an ASP.NET Web Application, giving the solution's folder, and then choosing MVC Application. This provides you with a simple MVC application that functions exactly as it is. Later on, you can alter it to make it uniquely yours. The web application should now be published to the Azure website that we developed.

- Launch Visual Studio and open your web application. Choose Publish Web Site with a right-click on the website. It will show the Publish Web dialog.
- Choose Web Sites for Windows Azure. A prompt to log into your Azure account will appear.
- You will be asked to choose which website to deploy after logging in. Click OK after choosing your website from the drop-down menu. It shows the connection details after retrieving the publishing settings from Azure.

78

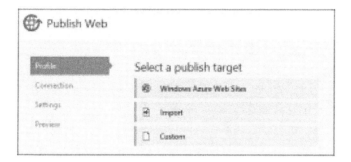

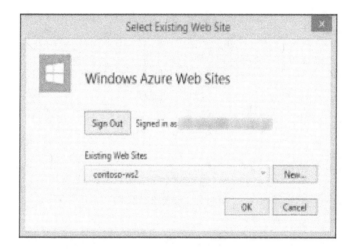

- To confirm that the connection is operational, click Validate Connection.
- To proceed to the following screen, where you can choose between Debug and Release Configuration, click Next.

- Click Next to proceed to the last screen after accepting the defaults on that one.

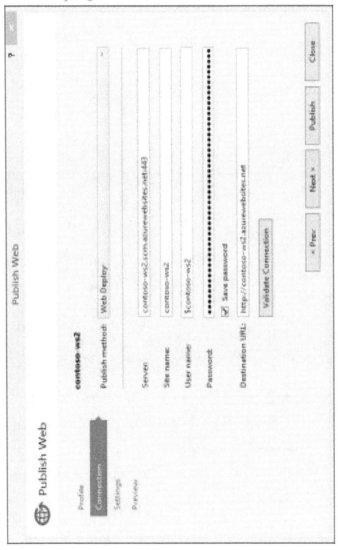

80

- You can view a preview of the files that will be published on the last screen. To publish the website, click Publish.

- After all the files have been deployed to the website, the website will open.

- When you make modifications to your website and follow the same procedure to publish it, Once more, only the files that have been added or altered will be published.

HOW TO TRACK A WEBSITE

A website might have a lot of metrics set up to be tracked.

- Enter the Azure Management Portal (manage(dot)windowsazure(dot)com)

- Choose WEBSITES, and then pick your website to accomplish this.

- Choose MONITOR from the options at the top of the screen when the Quick Start or DASHBOARD appears.

- CPU Time, Data In, Data Out, HTTP Server Errors, and Requests are the only six metrics that are displayed at first. The response times are also displayed here if you have Endpoint Monitoring configured on the CONFIGURE page.

81

The previously set endpoints for San Jose, California, Hong Kong, and Dublin are visible. Only six metrics can be chosen to show on the chart at any given time, but you can request as many metrics as you need to be shown in the list.

- By selecting +ADD METRICS at the bottom of the 65, you may add metrics screen. A number of additional options are available for selection.

- The time period that is shown is one hour, as chosen in the top-right corner. Take note that the y-axis is absent. This is due to the fact that every statistic has a unique y-axis value, which is charted to maximize the available space.

- Other monitoring apps, such as App Dynamics and New Relic, are accessible via the Azure Store in the Azure Management Portal. In the Developer Analytics area, they can be chosen and set up on the CONFIGURE screen.

CLOUD SERVICES VIA PAAS

The term "cloud service" has two meanings in Azure. One is to serve as a container for virtual machines (VMs) that you design and manage yourself. For instance, you could make

82

four identical virtual machines and place them in a single cloud service. After that, you would use the cloud service's IP address as the entry point, and Azure would automatically balance the load between the four virtual machines. You must deploy the application to each virtual machine (VM) if you wish to update the one that is currently executing on those VMs. To guarantee that you always have a minimum number of virtual machines available, you can include them in an availability set. You have to manually add or delete virtual machines (VMs) from the cloud service, as well as stop and start them, if you wish to scale the application up or down.

The second type of cloud service is one where Azure takes care of managing and maintaining your virtual machines. Simply publish a new version of the application to update all the virtual machines (VMs). Azure will update each VM, cycling through them to ensure there is no downtime. To modify the quantity of virtual machines (VMs), simply go the Azure Management Portal and adjust the instance count. Azure will then add or remove the desired number of VMs on your behalf.

The second type of cloud service is covered. You have worker roles or web roles in these cloud services. The main

83

distinction between the two is that IIS is installed by default in web roles. Web applications, WCF services, and anything else that needs IIS are often handled by web roles. Worker roles are typically utilized for continuous processing. For instance, you may have messages in a queue that you would like to process. In an endless loop, the worker role looks for messages in the queue, retrieves them, and processes them if they are discovered. As a worker, you can process a lot of files, videos, photos, etc.

HOW TO SET UP A CLOUD SERVICE

Let's build a web role for a cloud service. After that, we may examine the settings and determine how to publish it.

- Create a new project in Visual Studio by selecting FILE > NEW PROJECT. Choose Windows Azure Cloud Service for the project type.

- Enter the solution's name and select OK. (You must install the Azure SDK and Tools if Windows Azure Cloud Service is not listed among your projects.) You will next be asked to choose your role or roles.

- To move the ASP.NET Web Role to the right, select it and click the arrow pointing to the right. If you would want to change the name of your web role, hover over it, click the pencil, and then click OK. You

84

will be asked to choose the type of ASP.NET project
you want to work on because you chose an ASP.NET

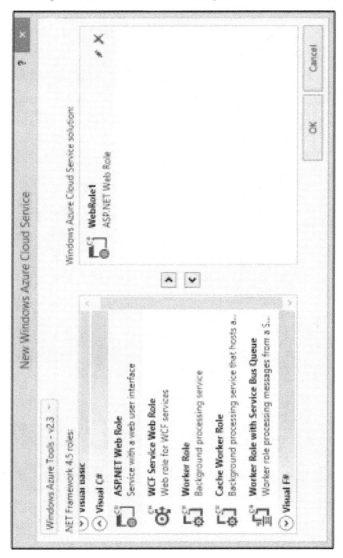

Web project. Click OK to proceed after selecting MVC.

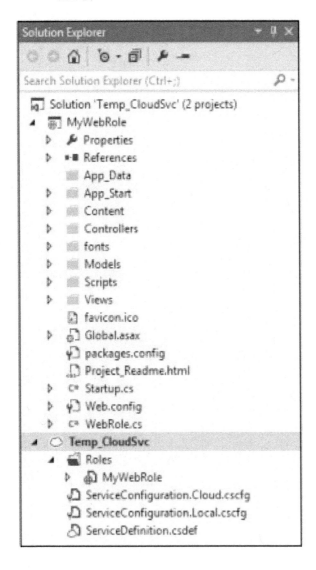

Upon reviewing your solution, you will notice that shows both the project with the cloud service and the project with the web role (MVC application). Observe that WebRole.cs is present in the web application project. This is what happens when the Azure web role spins up. This is left empty by default, but you can add event handlers for the role's startup and shutdown. If you plan to use an Azure queue, for instance, you may want to include code in the role initialization to check for the queue's existence and establish it if it doesn't.

You can access the role's properties by double-clicking on it. The following are a few of the most often utilized properties: Configuration parameters include storage connection strings, diagnostics setup, instance count, and virtual machine size. The service level agreement (SLA) requires a minimum instance count of two in order to be eligible. Configuration settings that are retrievable by code. While the website is active, these can be changed in the Azure Management Portal. It is possible to have options for both debug and release setups.

87

Endpoints An HTTP endpoint will be open by default for a web role. You can open alternative endpoints, like HTTPS, and change that.

Local Data Storage Local storage can be set up for every instance. For instance, you might set up a 5 GB SSD to be used for temporary files here. Every instance would possess a 5 GB local resource space of its own. Certifications Here, you can set up certificates to be used for Remote Desktop (RDP) and SSL access. The certificate needs to be uploaded to the Azure Management Portal as well.

The ServiceConfiguration.*.cscfg file(s) contains the settings in XML format. osFamily and osVersion are two XML properties in the file that are not visible through the user interface. The operating system that will operate in the virtual machine is chosen by osFamily. For instance, Windows Server 2012 R2 is osFamily 4, Windows Server 2012 is osFamily 3, and Windows Server SP2 is osFamily 2.

Leave the variables at their existing defaults, osFamily = 4 and osVersion = *, unless your application calls for a different version. The most recent version of the chosen osFamily will be used, as indicated by the asterisk in osVersion.

88

Multiple ServiceConfiguration.*.cscfg files are possible. It will ask which one you wish to use when you publish. The ServiceDefinition.csdef file is the only one present. This contains the endpoint definitions and the master list of configuration setting variables. It has the instance size as well. The sizes of instances vary from A9 (16 CPU cores, 112 GB memory) to Extra Small (shared, 1 CPU core, 768 MB RAM). With a greater memory-to-core ratio, a Solid State Drive (SSD) for the temporary drive, and faster CPUs, the new D-series virtual machine is also available. See —Virtual Machine and Cloud Service Sizes for Azure.

The storage and compute emulators can be used to evaluate a cloud service. As part of the Azure SDK and Tools, these are installed. By designating the cloud service as your beginning project, you may simply press F5 to launch the emulator or emulators and launch the application in your preferred browser.

HOW TO MAKE A CLOUD SERVICE PUBLIC

Let's make our cloud service from the last part public.

- Launch Visual Studio and open the solution.
- You must first build a cloud service on the portal before publishing your cloud service for the first time.

89

Jason Taylor

- To accomplish this, click CLOUD SERVICES in the left column after logging into the Azure Management Portal (manage(dot)windowsazure(dot)com).

- Click +NEW > CLOUD SERVICE > QUICK CREATE at the bottom of the page. A window asking for the URL and REGION will appear. Every cloud service must have a different URL. Keep in mind that cloudapp.net will be the domain of the URL.

- Click CREATE CLOUD SERVICE after choosing a nearby region. Your cloud service will be created by Azure. There are currently no instances for this; Azure will launch the instances, install your application, and then Give them access.

- Right-click the cloud service project in Visual Studio and choose Publish. The Microsoft account you use for Azure will be asked for; enter it. The Publish Windows Azure Application window now displays your subscription. To access the Settings screen, click Next.

90

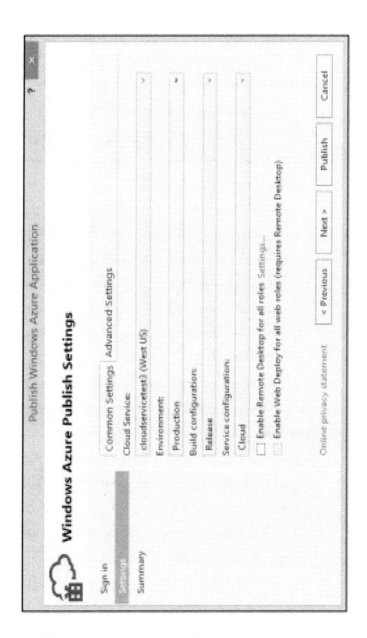

- Using the interface, pick the cloud service you just added. You can choose between Production and Staging for the Environment (more on that later).

- Choose a Build Configuration of Debug if you plan to debug remotely; if not, choose Release. A list of Visual Studio configurations is called the Service Configuration.

- You might have one for development, one for staging, and one for production, and you could choose which one to use here. This one display Cloud and Local. In a cloud service, this is a useful technique to accommodate several environments with varied configuration options (such database connection strings).

- You can assign a deployment label here. You may include a version number in this box, for instance. The date and time can also be added to the deployment label. This will help you determine when it was last deployed and will be visible to you on the portal.

- The package that is uploaded for you is kept in the storage account. The data in the package is used to construct the instances. There are two files in the bundle. One is a configuration file that specifies the

92

program configuration, and the other is the zipped copies of the application assemblies.

- Click Next after accepting the default settings.

- This will bring up a summary screen with all of your choices and allow you to save this publishing profile for later use. Click Publish once the publishing profile has been saved.

- A Windows Azure Activity Log window will popup in Visual Studio, showing the deployment's progress. After the storage account has been verified, the package will be uploaded, instances with the appropriate operating system will be created and started, your software will be installed, and the application will be made available. This requires five to ten minutes. When publishing is finished, the activity window will show.

- You can open your website in your preferred browser by clicking on the URL.

- You may also use Visual Studio to generate the deployment package for your cloud service by right-clicking on the cloud project, choosing Package, and then publishing your service. There are two files in the bundle. One is a configuration file that specifies

93

the program configuration, and the other is the zipped copies of the application assemblies.

- After that, you may either choose the STAGING environment and choose UPLOAD, or you can go to the site and UPDATE on PRODUCTION.

- You can upload the package in this way, and Azure will perform the same function as if you were publishing from Visual Studio. Instead of having Visual Studio do everything for you, you only need to manually complete the upload package. If packages are created by one group and then deployed to staging or production by another, you might wish to do this.

HOW TO GROW AND KEEP AN EYE ON A CLOUD SERVICE

Setting the VM Size and Instance count in the service configuration and then republishing is the simplest method of scaling a cloud service.

Using the scaling options in the Azure Management Portal (manage(dot)windowsazure(dot)com) is an additional method. After logging into the site, let's examine the PaaS cloud service's features.

94

- Click CLOUD SERVICES in the left column after logging in.

- It should be noted that the PaaS cloud services and the cloud services you build as a wrapper to one or more virtual machines (VMs), which were covered at the beginning of this section, are shown here in the same list.

- In the preceding section, choose the cloud service that you developed and made public.

CHAPTER FOUR

OPTIONS FOR SCALE

This is how it is done:

- Select the SCALE option to scale a cloud service.

The alternatives are as follows:

SCHEDULED TIMES FOR SCALE

- Click Set Up Schedule Times to make use of this function. The scheduling times screen appears as a result.
- You can choose the start and end times for a day as well as the scale settings for weekdays versus weekends and day against night.
- Additionally, you can designate the start and finish hours of the scale for particular dates.

METRICS OF SCALE

CPU or Queue Whether scaling by CPU or QUEUE, many of the options are the same.

- You choose the target CPU that will cause the scaling event when scaling by CPU. For instance, when the CPU % is between 60 and 80 percent, you might want it to scale.

96

- You choose the storage account, queue name, and the maximum number of messages that each instance

97

may process when scaling by queue. The number of instances required can be calculated by dividing the total number of messages in the queue by the number of messages that each instance can handle.

- It will attempt to scale to this figure or, if smaller, to the maximum number of instances. It will scale up to the maximum number of instances or four instances {2,000 messages divided by (500 messages/instance) = 4}, whichever is smaller, for instance, if you set this to 500 and 2,000 messages arrive.

- When scaling by queue, the queue and queue target are set. You can alter the instance range for both choices. This is the number of instances you wish to have, both minimum and maximum.

ACCOUNT OR NAMESPACE	[Select Scope] ⌄
QUEUE NAME	[Select Queue] ⌄
TARGET PER MACHINE	2000

You can choose how many instances to scale in or out with each autoscale event for both choices, as well as how long to wait before scaling again. You might wish to scale out two instances at a time, for instance, but no more frequently than once every 20 minutes. You may want to scale down one

99

instance at a time, but not more than once per half hour, just in case the activity spikes up again. With each scaling operation, the number of instances to scale up or down is set. It's vital to keep in mind that the autoscale event takes around an hour to occur because the monitoring framework reads data that is 45 minutes averaged and is roughly 15 minutes behind. An autoscaling event requires a sustained CPU spike; a rise to 75% and then a sharp decline will not cause an autoscaling event.

100

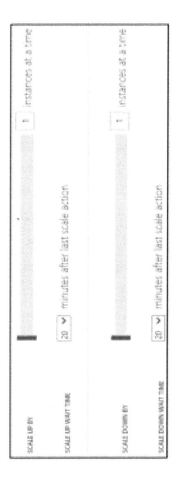

HOW TO TRACK

A cloud service's performance can be tracked in two ways. One is via Visual Studio, and the other is via the Azure Management Portal (MONITOR tab). Navigate to the cloud service's MONITOR tab in the portal, then select

101

+METRICS at the bottom of the page. Only a small set of metrics are accessible.

You can add a lot more performance metrics to MONITOR by going to the CONFIGURE tab, changing the monitoring level to VERBOSE, and then clicking +METRICS in MONITOR once more. Azure will create tables in Azure Storage with names like WAD[deploymentid]PT1HRTable that contain 5-minute, 1-hour, and 12-hour averages. The duration of data retention can be specified in days. Performance metrics can also be added using Visual Studio. Select the Configuration tab after opening your solution and going to the cloud service properties. You will discover that a Custom Diagnostics plan can be defined;

Diagnostics

☑ Enable Diagnostics

○ Errors only

○ All information

● Custom plan   Edit...

102

- Click Edit after choosing Custom Plan to get the Diagnostics configuration. There are numerous additional metrics that you can put on the Performance Counters tab. You can even include performance counters that aren't in the list.

- Approximately every five minutes, these diagnostics are written as point-in-time values to the WADPerformanceCounterTable table. This data does not have an automatic retention period; it will remain in the table until you delete it. Since the deployment ID is included in the table name of the other tables and it varies every time a cloud service is deployed, I advise utilizing the Visual Studio configuration out of the two possibilities.

- This implies that you must search every table if you wish to graph your metrics over time. All of the metrics are kept in a single table if you make the modifications in Visual Studio, which facilitates querying the data over time.

103

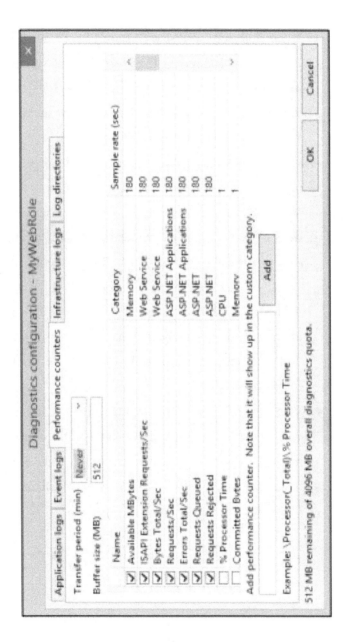

The image shows a "Diagnostics configuration - MyWebRole" dialog with tabs: Application logs, Event logs, Performance counters, Infrastructure logs, Log directories.

Transfer period (min): Never
Buffer size (MB): 512

Name	Category	Sample rate (sec)
☑ Available MBytes	Memory	180
☑ ISAPI Extension Requests/Sec	Web Service	180
☑ Bytes Total/Sec	Web Service	180
☑ Requests/Sec	ASP.NET Applications	180
☑ Errors Total/Sec	ASP.NET Applications	180
☑ Requests Queued	ASP.NET	180
☑ Requests Rejected	ASP.NET	180
☐ % Processor Time	CPU	1
☐ Committed Bytes	Memory	1

Add performance counter. Note that it will show up in the custom category.

[Add]

Example: \Processor(_Total)\% Processor Time

512 MB remaining of 4096 MB overall diagnostics quota.

[OK] [Cancel]

104

OTHER POINTS

Here are some things to remember:

PORTAL CONFIGURATION

The Azure Management Portal's CONFIGURE tab allows you to change the operating system family and version. You can modify and save configuration settings in the portal if you have any in your worker or web role. The original package that was submitted to Azure is unaltered in both of these situations. This implies that the manual modifications you made via the portal will be erased if Azure applies fixes to your virtual machines and then restarts them. Therefore, make sure to update the Visual Studio solution and deploy a new version after making these modifications through the portal.

THE PORTAL'S PRODUCTION AND STAGING SLOTS

Every cloud service has a time window for both production and staging. The designated URL, such as yourgreatwebapp.cloudapp.net, is used during the production slot. Every time you deploy a new package to the staging slot, a globally unique identifier (GUID) for the URL is assigned to it. Because of this, testing entangled cloud services—like A calls B calls C—becomes challenging.

105

Either the addresses in A that point to B and B that point to C must be changed, or the DNS records must be changed, which may take some time to take effect.

Using the Azure Management Portal to configure several cloud services for a single web application is one workaround for this. For instance, you may configure stMyWebApp for staging and MyWebApp for production. Do your testing after publishing to stage. By publishing to MyWebApp's staging slot and performing a VIP Swap—which switches the IP addresses for the two deployment slots—you may successfully put the new one into production when you're ready to put the modifications into production. Remember to remove the previous one from the staging slot!

ROLES OF WORKERS

Right-click the Roles and choose Add New Worker Role Project to include a worker role in your cloud project. Messages are typically retrieved from a queue, processed, and then removed from the queue using worker roles.

A online application that allows users to upload images is a nice illustration of this. You post a message to the queue after the upload is finished because you want to resize the images. The worker role would delete the message from the queue after retrieving it, resizing the images, and placing them in the destination folder.

PLATFORM-AS-A-SERVICE (PAAS) FOR AZURE VIRTUAL MACHINES

Platform-as-a-Service (PaaS) for Azure Virtual Machines is unquestionably a desirable choice for a particular class of applications. But not all solutions should or can be incorporated into the PaaS model. Operating system configuration, disk durability, the ability to install and operate conventional server applications, and other tasks necessitate almost complete control over the infrastructure. This is where Azure Virtual Machines and Infrastructure-as-a-Service (IaaS) are useful.

AZURE VIRTUAL MACHINES: WHAT ARE THEY?

Along with virtual networks, one of the key components of Azure's IaaS capabilities is Azure Virtual Machines. Windows Server or Linux virtual machines (VMs) can be installed in a Microsoft Azure datacenter using Azure Virtual Machines. You are in complete control of the virtual machine's configuration. Installing, configuring, and maintaining all server software as well as operating system patches is under your purview.

107

Take note It can be a bit challenging to understand the terms used to refer to a virtual machine instance and the Azure Virtual Machines functionality. As a result, Azure Virtual Machines will be used to refer to the functionality throughout this chapter, whereas virtual machine, or VM, will refer to an instance of a real computing node.

Control and persistence are the two main distinctions between Azure Virtual Machines and Azure Cloud Services (i.e., web and worker roles). You can concentrate on developing the application rather than maintaining the server architecture by using PaaS cloud services, which are mainly maintained by the Azure platform and comprise web and/or worker roles, as covered in Chapter 2, "Azure Websites and Azure Cloud Services." You are in charge of almost every aspect of an Azure virtual machine (VM).

Although Azure virtual machines (VMs) are stateful servers with persistent disks, web and worker roles are typically regarded as stateless (mostly because they lack a persistent disk). Disks come in two varieties: OS disks and data disks. The data disk is optional, but the operating system disk is necessary. We'll go into more detail about these drives later in this chapter, but for now, just know that the OS disk

108

houses your operating system (Windows or Linux) and the data disk houses your application data.

Because of the level of control afforded to the user and the use of persistent disks, VMs are ideal for a wide range of server workloads that do not fit into a PaaS model. The Microsoft Azure platform makes it feasible to execute server workloads including database servers (SQL Server, Oracle, MongoDB, and so forth), Windows Server Active Directory, SharePoint, and many more. If desired, users can move such workloads from an on-premises datacenter to one or more Azure regions, a process often called lift and shift.

Before continuing much further, it is important to understand a little more about what truly makes up an Azure cloud service. Fundamentally, a cloud service is a container for virtual machines. The container provides several key features, including a DNS endpoint, network connectivity (including from the public Internet if desired), security, and a unit of management. A cloud service can hold multiple VM types: Azure web and worker role instances or Azure Virtual Machines VMs. As of the time of this writing, a cloud service container cannot simultaneously contain both web and worker role instances and Azure Virtual Machines VMs (that is, a cloud service cannot host PaaS and IaaS VMs at

109

the same time). An Azure cloud service contains either a collection of web and worker roles or VMs.

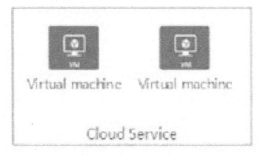

110

When you're done, click the blue Create button to tell Azure to begin building your virtual machine (which may take a

111

few minutes). Remote Desktop is enabled by default when you create a virtual machine (VM) through the Azure Preview Portal. To connect to the VM, click the Connect button on top of the desired VM blade. This will start a download of a preconfigured Remote Desktop (.rdp) file to your local computer. Open the RDP file and connect to the VM. You will need to enter the administrative user name and password that were set when you first provisioned the VM.

HOW TO SET UP DISKS

Azure Virtual Machines are created using VHD files. Azure Virtual Machines employ two different kinds of VHDs: Picture a VHD that serves as a blueprint for building a fresh Azure virtual machine. It lacks settings like an administrative user, machine name, and so on because it is a template. Later in this chapter, there is more information on how to create and use photos. The disk a bootable VHD that

112

can be utilized as a virtual machine's mountable drive. An image becomes a disk when it has been provided. Disks come in two varieties: OS disks and data disks. Page blobs in Azure Storage serve as a backup for all persistent disks, including the OS and data disks. As a result, the disks gain the advantages of blob storage, including geo-redundancy options, durability, and high availability. Blob storage offers a way to securely store data for the virtual machine to use. On the virtual machine, the disks can be mounted as drives.

To avoid unintentionally deleting the page blob that contains the VHD, the associated container, or the storage account, the Azure platform will maintain an indefinite lease on the page blob. As the name implies, an OS disk is utilized for the operating system. The OS disk, where Windows stores its data, is the standard C drive for a Windows Server virtual machine. It is utilized for the root directory's /dev/sda1 partition in a Linux virtual machine. For Windows, the maximum size of an OS drive is presently 127 GB.

Data disks are the other kind of disk that Azure Virtual Machines employ. Additionally, the data disk is utilized for holding a variety of data, just as the name would imply. The maximum size of each data disk is 1 TB. program data, such

113

that from your custom program, or server software, like SQL Server and its associated data and log files, are frequently stored on the data drives. A physical temporary disk that is not persisted to Azure Storage is also included in Azure Virtual Machines. Only temporary (or duplicated) data should be stored on the temporary drive; otherwise, the data will be lost in the case of a hardware failure. The many disk types are depicted

CACHING

The OS and data drives can be cached by Azure Virtual Machines. For some workloads, caching can enhance speed and possibly decrease transactions to Azure storage. Read/Write, Read, and None are the three choices for the disk cache.

Read/Write (default) and Read are the two cache settings available on the OS disk. Three cache settings are available on the data disk: **Read/Write**, **Read**, and **None (default)**. Be advised that there is currently a cap of four data disks with caching enabled when building a virtual machine (VM) or adding disks to an already-existing VM.

114

CONNECT A DISK

You can either upload an existing VHD or start with a fresh,

empty drive to add a data disk to the virtual machine. The Azure Preview Portal can be used for either.

You can attach an existing VHD to the virtual machine (VM) by uploading it to Azure. You can use Windows' Disk Management to build a VHD if you don't already have one. You can view how many disks are connected to the current virtual machine (VM) and the total size of all the associated disks from the Disks lens The Disks blade must first be opened by clicking on the Disks lens in order to create and

115

attach a new disk. You can either attach an existing disk or a new disk to this blade.

- Click Attach New at the top of the Disks blade to add a new disk.

FROM THE OUTCOME

By attaching a new disk blade, you can adjust a number of important settings:

- **Container for Storage**: Your new data disk will be stored in a blob container and an Azure Storage account.
- **Name of the disk file**: You can either supply your own or accept the default.
- **Sizes (GB)**: The new data disk's (VHD) size.
- **Caching of the Host**: The data disk's cache choice to employ.

Click Attach Existing at the top of the Disks blade to attach an existing data disk. The Attach An Existing Disc blade that results will provide you the choice to choose an existing VHD from your Azure Storage account. An existing VHD can be uploaded to a blob container in the selected storage account using your preferred Azure Storage management

116

tool (make sure the VHD is specified as a page blob and not a block blob).

DISK FORMATTING

Similar to a drive on a real Windows server, each data disk must be formatted after being connected to the Azure virtual machine. The VHDs are stored in a sparse fashion utilizing page blobs in Azure Storage. This indicates that Azure

Storage fees only apply to data that has been written to the VHD. It is advised that you format the disks using a fast format as a result. Large ranges of zeros won't be stored with the page blob in a fast manner, saving you money and actual storage space.

Use Remote Desktop to connect to the virtual machine remotely in order to format the disk or disks. Open Disk Management after connecting and logging onto the virtual machine. You may see the disks and format any unallocated disks using the native Windows tool Disk Management. To continue, right-click the unallocated drive and choose Initialize drive.

To initialize the disk, finish the wizard. You can start formatting the disk after it has been initialized.

- Choose New Simple Volume from the menu when you right-click the disk. It should launch the New Simple Volume Wizard.
- Choose the preferred drive letter and volume size as you proceed through the process.
- Make sure to choose Perform A Quick Format when the volume formatting option is displayed.

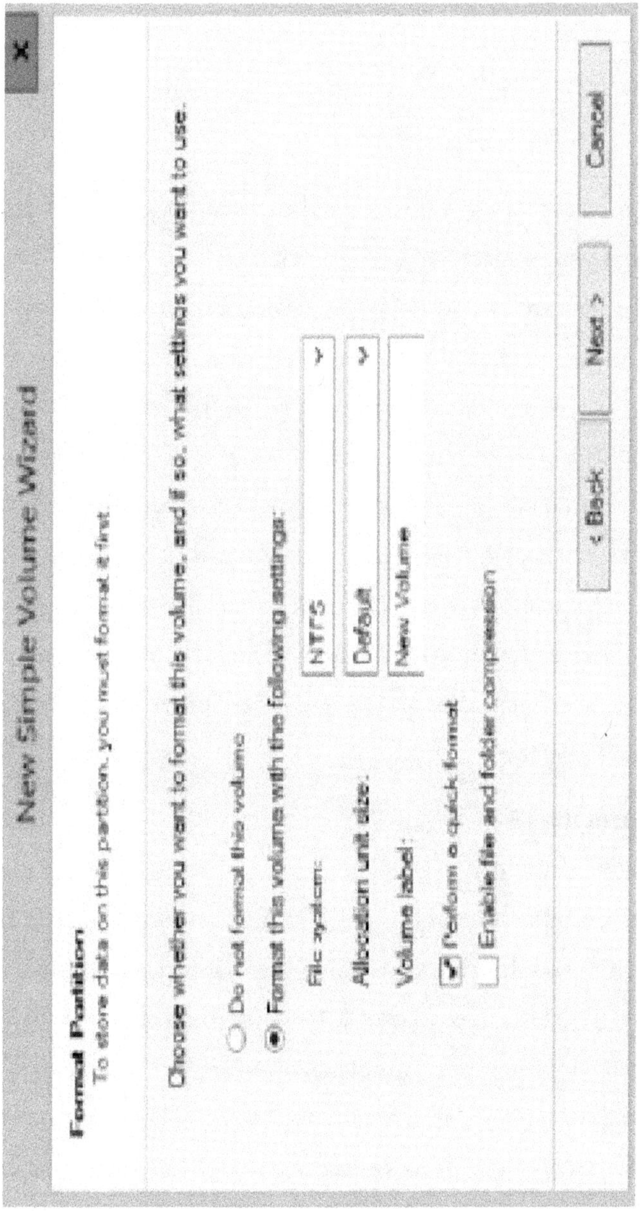
New Simple Volume Wizard
Format Partition
To store data on this partition, you must format it first.
Choose whether you want to format this volume, and if so, what settings you want to use.
Do not format this volume
Format this volume with the following settings:
File system:
NTFS
Allocation unit size:
Default
Volume label:
New Volume
Perform a quick format
Enable file and folder compression
< Back
Next >
Cancel

119

- To begin formatting the disk, complete the wizard's steps.

Disk performance IOPS is an additional consideration for Azure virtual machine drives. Each data drive has a limit of 500 IOPS and 60 MB/s (for Standard-tier virtual machines) as of this writing. For the intended workload, this may or may not be enough. To make sure the disk performance is adequate, you should do performance tests. If not, think about utilizing storage spaces (Windows Server 2012 or later) or stripping the disk to improve disk performance. The disk configuration requirements are universal across a wide range of workloads, despite the fact that the whitepaper in question is unique to running SQL Server on an Azure virtual machine.

ENDPOINTS

Endpoints for an Azure cloud service are made public by the **Azure Load Balancer.** Using a related protocol (such TCP or UDP) on the virtual machine, the Azure Load Balancer setup regulates how requests from the Internet arrive at a particular port. Azure virtual machines are by default unable to receive requests from the Internet. A virtual machine must be set up with one or more endpoints in order to accomplish

120

this. By mapping public ports on the Azure Load Balancer to private ports on the virtual machine, this configuration essentially sets up the Azure Load Balancer to accept Internet traffic.

Locate the Endpoints lens at the bottom of the Virtual Machine blade and scroll down to inspect or update, including adding endpoints for a VM. The current endpoints, along with their names and matching ports, are displayed there.

A load-balanced setup for a collection of virtual machines can also be made. By doing this, you can make several virtual machines (VMs) function as a group of web servers in a web farm setting, for instance. Instead of sending incoming requests to a single virtual machine, the Azure Load Balancer will divide them across the available VMs when the load-balanced setting is in place.

To view more information about the current endpoints, including the ability to add new endpoints or remove existing ones, pick the Endpoints lens. This opens a new blade. When you add an endpoint, the Azure Load Balancer is told to permit Internet traffic to reach your virtual machine (VM) over the specified protocol and port. You may need to set up the server's firewall to permit traffic on the specified

121

port and protocol if your virtual machine is running its own

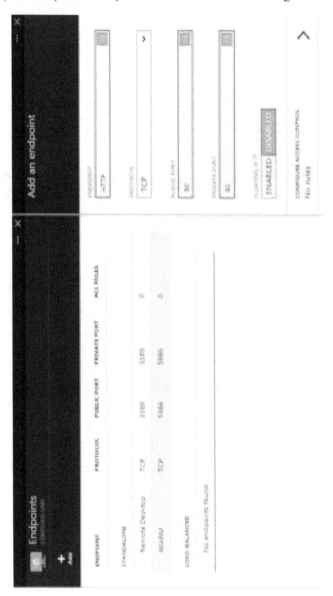

firewall program, such as Windows Firewall for Windows Server instances.

MANAGEMENT OF VIRTUAL MACHINES

Setting up an Azure virtual machine is just the first step. You should take into account a number of crucial elements in order to effectively administer the virtual machines. It's crucial to take into account elements like scalability, SLA, disk management, and machine maintenance.

The user is primarily in charge of managing the virtual machines overall. The virtual machine will be externally accessible thanks to the Microsoft Azure platform. You can do almost anything you want as the user aside from that. PowerShell or a regular Remote Desktop connection can be used to remotely configure and operate the virtual machine.

SET OF AVAILABILITY

Physical servers housed in Microsoft's Azure datacenters are home to Azure virtual machines. The possibility of a failure exists, just like with the majority of physical devices. The Azure virtual machines that are housed on the actual server will likewise fail if it does. The Azure platform will make a swift effort to locate a healthy host server on which to rebuild the virtual machine in the event of a failure. It can take a few minutes for this service to heal. The program or applications

123

running in that virtual machine will not be accessible during that period.

In addition to hardware malfunctions, recurring updates started by the Azure platform itself may potentially have an impact on the virtual machines. You are still in charge of patching the operating system of the guest virtual machine that you build, but Microsoft will upgrade the host operating system that the guest virtual machines run on on a regular basis. The virtual machine will be rebooted during these updates, making it momentarily unavailable. At least two instances of the virtual machine should be deployed in order to prevent a single point of failure. Actually, Azure only offers a service level agreement (SLA) when two or more virtual machines are placed into an availability set. During a host operating system upgrade in the datacenter, this logical feature makes sure that a collection of linked virtual machines (VMs) is deployed so that they are not all susceptible to a single point of failure and are not all upgraded simultaneously. To prevent a single point of failure from affecting both of them at once, the first two virtual machines (VMs) that are deployed in an availability set are assigned to two distinct fault domains. In a similar vein, the Azure platform minimizes the impact when it imposes host operating system changes one update

124

domain at a time by allocating the first five virtual machines (VMs) deployed in each availability set to five distinct update domains. Virtual machines (VMs) in an availability set ought to carry out the same set of tasks.

Sidebar: Domains of faults and virtual machine updates By viewing the associated cloud service in the Azure Management Portal at

http://manage(dot)windowsazure(dot)com, you can see the update and fault domains utilized for your virtual machines. The sixth virtual machine is positioned in update domain 0, while the preceding five are each in a separate updated domain. VMs, update domains, and fault domains. As part of the VM provisioning procedure, the virtual machine (VM) can be added to an existing availability set. It will be necessary to build an availability set if one does not already exist. Choose the Availability Set lens on the blade of the appropriate virtual machine to set its availability.

Then, at the top of the Availability Set blade, select New. Enter the desired name for the new availability set on the New Availability Set blade that is produced. It is possible to add an existing virtual machine (VM) to an availability set if it isn't already there. But the virtual machine needs to belong to the same cloud service (it needs

125

to have the same DNS name, like contoso.cloudapp.net). Navigate to the Availability Set lens after selecting the preferred virtual machine. Choose the preferred existing availability set from there. To apply the update, the virtual machine will restart.

AGREEMENT ON SERVICE LEVEL

Microsoft provides a 99.95 percent connection SLA for multiple instance virtual machines (VMs) installed in an availability set as of this writing. This implies that at least two instances of the virtual machine (VM) must be deployed inside an availability set in order for the SLA to be applicable. Also See For complete information, view the SLA at http://azure(dot)microsoft(dot)com/en-us/support/legal/sla/.

SCALABILITY

Azure Virtual Machines, like the majority of Azure services, are scaled out rather than scaled up. This indicates that adding bigger, more potent computers is not as desirable as deploying additional instances of the same setup. VMs must be positioned within an availability set before they can be scaled (in or out). Determining the maximum number of virtual machines (VMs) is crucial when choosing a scale-out strategy for them, as they need to be built, configured, and added to an availability set. The VMs in the availability set are employed to meet the scale-out requirements when the time comes. For Azure's autoscale functionality to work, all of the virtual machines (VMs) in an availability set must have the same size.

As of this writing, you must use the Azure Management Portal at http://manage(dot)windowsazure(dot)com in order to utilize Azure's autoscale functionality for virtual machines in an availability set. The Azure Preview Portal, located at http://portal.azure.com, will soon have the capability to scale virtual machines.

The Scale area of the Azure Management Portal offers the ability to automatically scale in or out the number of virtual machines (VMs) within a service. Azure manages scaling automatically using the configuration rules that are supplied. For Azure Storage queues or Service Bus, the configuration can be tied to metrics like average CPU utilization or queue depth (number of messages in the queue), or it can be tied to the time of day (e.g., scale out during business hours and contract in the evening). The average usage during the preceding hour is the average CPU utilization %. Azure uses the desired number of messages to be processed per machine

127

as the metric for queue depth. This means that when

determining if a scaling action should be taken, Azure will divide the total number of messages in a queue by the number of instances. When the scalability conditions are satisfied, Azure will automatically scale in about an hour.

This covers the time required to provision a new virtual machine as well as the time spent gathering VM metric data. Therefore, the default autoscale rules are probably not appropriate for rapid burst scale-out requirements, but they are frequently good for macro level scaling.

The CPU utilization scaling settings will make an effort to maintain the average CPU utilization % for all instances within the specified range. You have control over the target range of virtual machines (VMs) and the criteria that determine when they will scale in or out. To guarantee that you never have too few or too many virtual machines (VMs), you can specify the minimum and maximum number that can be utilized. Azure will scale in or out in accordance with the number of virtual machines specified for when a scaling action should take place, should one be required. Keep in mind that every scaling operation has a wait time, often known as a "cooldown" phase. By doing this, the system is kept from crashing virtual machines and is given time to try to settle before implementing another scaling measure.

129

Jason Taylor

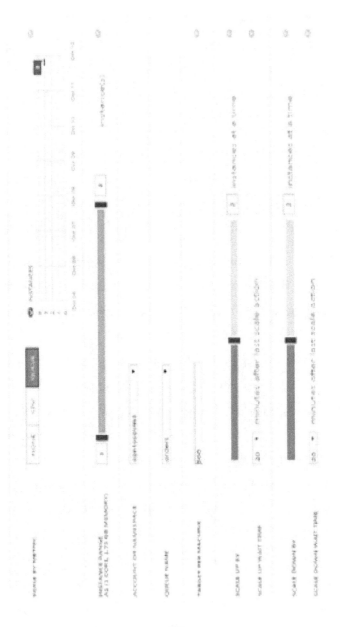

130

The queue utilization parameters are essentially the same as the CPU utilization settings. The statistic to utilize is the quantity of messages in a particular Azure Storage or Service Bus queue, rather than deciding on a scale based on typical CPU utilization. It is, more precisely, the desired quantity of messages that a virtual machine ought to process. By dividing the total number of messages by the desired messages per VM, Azure will automatically modify the number of virtual machines. Azure will try to scale up to four virtual machines (VMs) based on the scale-up rule and wait time, for instance, if the aim is 500 messages per VM and there are 2,000 messages in the queue.

Remember that the service can only scale out until the subscription's core limit is met. This implies that the virtual machines (VMs) being launched cannot use more than 20 cores overall if the subscription has a 20-core restriction.

HOW TO CAPTURE AN IMAGE

After your new Azure virtual machine is set up the way you want it, you may wish to make a clone of it. For instance, you may wish to use the virtual machine you just created as a template to construct multiple additional VMs. The term "capturing the VM" or "creating a generalized VM Image" describes this procedure. Along with the OS disk, any

131

associated data disks are also captured while creating a virtual machine image.

Because the original VM (the original source) is erased once the capture is finished, you will no longer be able to use it when you capture the VM to use as a template for subsequent VMs. Alternatively, you can utilize a template picture in the Azure Management Portal's Virtual Machine gallery. To capture a virtual machine (VM) and make it usable as a template picture, you must follow a few procedures. Only the Azure Management Portal, located at http://manage.windowsazure.com, supports capturing virtual machines (VMs) as of this writing. The instructions listed below pertain to capturing a Windows virtual machine server. Waagent -deprovision would be used in place of a Windows sysprep command, but otherwise the procedure would be the same if you were operating a Linux virtual machine.

- As mentioned previously in this chapter, use Remote Desktop to connect to the virtual machine.
- As the administrator, launch a command prompt window.
- Launch Sysprep.exe after navigating to the %windir%/system32/sysprep directory.

132

Take the following steps in the System Preparation Tool:

- Choose Enter System Out-Of-Box Experience (OOBE) from the System Cleanup Action list. Check the box for "Generalize." Choose Shutdown from the drop-down list of Shutdown Options.

- Sysprep will run in the VM. When the virtual machine starts to shut down, you will be disconnected if you are still using RDP to access it. Observe the virtual machine in the Azure Management Portal until it fully terminates and displays the status "Stopped."

- Click the CAPTURE button in the bottom tray menu after choosing the virtual machine to capture from the Azure Management Portal.

133

Jason Taylor

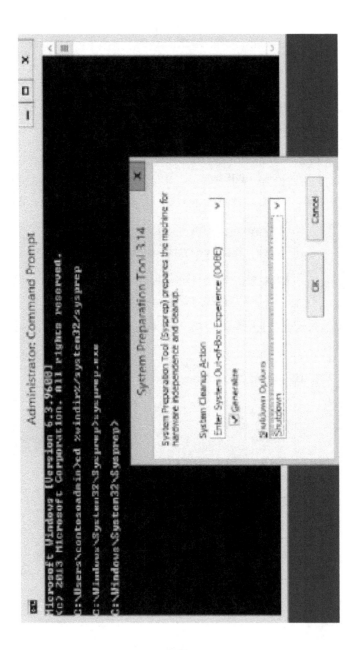

134

INSTANCES IMAGES DISKS

NAME	STATUS	SUBSCRIPTION	↑ LOCATION
centosd (linux vm1	▣ Stopped (Deallocated)	Windows Azure MVP MSDN Subs...	East US
rdr2020_vm3	☐ Stopped	Windows Azure MVP MSDN Subs...	East US
centron_vm5	▣ Stopped (Deallocated)	Windows Azure MVP MSDN Subs...	East US

CONNECT START SHUT DOWN ATTACH DETACH DISK CAPTURE DELETE

- Choose the I Have Run Sysprep On The Virtual Machine check box and give the new image a name.
- To take a picture, click the checkmark.
- The picture ought to now show up under My Images in your Virtual Machine gallery. This image can now be used to start a new virtual machine instance.

The procedure that was just explained is not the only option. You can make a customized virtual machine image if you want to take a picture of the virtual machine for any reason (for instance, you are about to install software that you are unsure will function). The OS disk and all connected data drives are included in a specialized virtual machine image, just like in a generalist one. When the new virtual machine is deployed, the disks are copied and handled as read-only disks. Simply choosing the required virtual machine (VM) in the Azure Management Portal and clicking CAPTURE will build a customized VM image. The sysprep procedure does not have to be followed. You run the risk of losing any data in memory when you attempt to capture a tailored virtual machine image while the machine is operating.

136

CHAPTER FIVE
STORAGE ON AZURE

A service run by Microsoft, Azure Storage offers scalable, redundant, and long-lasting storage. Microsoft handles all of your maintenance and backups. 50 storage accounts, each with a 500 TB capacity, can be hosted by an Azure subscription. Blob, File Share, Table, and Queue services are among the different kinds of services that Azure Storage offers. Each storage account has metrics that you can activate, and you can configure alerts to inform you when a particular statistic (like data outflow) gets out of control.

We describe each of them, explain their functions, and in certain situations, demonstrate how to handle them. As of this writing, a new feature called Premium Storage has just been launched. This new SSD-based storage type is built to handle workloads that require a lot of input and output.

STORAGE OF BLOBS

Blob is an abbreviation for binary big object. In essence, blobs are files similar to those you keep on your computer (or tablet, smartphone, etc.). They might be images, HTML files, Microsoft Excel files, virtual hard drives (VHDs), or just about anything else. Using URLs, the REST interface, or one of the Azure SDK storage client libraries, you can save files on the Azure Blob service and retrieve them from any location in the world. (A variety of languages, including .NET, Node.js, Java, PHP, Ruby, and Python, have storage client libraries available.) You must first create a storage account in order to use the Blob service. You can build containers, which are like folders, and then place blobs inside of them after you have a storage account. As long as the storage account doesn't exceed the 500 TB storage account capacity restriction, you can have an infinite number of containers and blobs in each container. Only a single-level hierarchy of containers is supported by the Blob service; that is, containers cannot be inside of other containers.

Block blobs and page blobs are the two types of blobs that Azure Storage offers. Ordinary files up to 200 GB in size are stored in block blobs. Block blobs are mostly used to store items that are read from start to finish, like media files or image files for websites. Because files greater than 64 MB must be uploaded as discrete blocks that are then combined (or committed) into the final blob, they are known as block blobs. Random-access files up to 1 TB in size are stored in page blobs. Page blobs are mostly utilized as the backup storage for the VHDs that supply robust disks for Azure Virtual Machines, which are an IaaS component of Azure Compute. Because they allow random read/write access to

138

512-byte pages, they are known as page blobs.

Blobs can be accessed by a URL, which looks like this:

http://[container]/[blobname]/blob(dot)core(dot)windows(dot)net/[storage account name]

There is just one physical level of containers supported by the Blob service. However, by permitting blob names to contain the '/' character, it facilitates the imitation of a file system with directories inside the containers. The ability to navigate this emulated file system is supported by the client APIs. For instance, if you wish to group the animals in a container named animals, you could add blobs named cats/tuxedo.png, cats/marmalade.png, and so on. The full blob name, including the subfolder, would be included in the URL.

Using a storage explorer tool, you can view the list of blobs as either a flat listing or a hierarchical directory tree. Cats would appear as a subdirectory under animals in the directory tree, along with the.png files included within. The blobs with their original names, cats/tuxedo.png and cats/marmalade.png, would be listed in the flat listing. Additionally, you can change the root of the URL by assigning a custom domain to the storage account, so you might have something like this:

[blobname]/[container]/[storage.companyname.com]

By using the company domain for both, you can avoid cross-domain problems when accessing files in blob storage from a website. To facilitate this kind of cross-source usage, blob storage additionally offers Cross-origin resource sharing (CORS).

FILES IN AZURE (PREVIEW)

Setting up highly available network file shares that are accessible via the common Server Message Block (SMB) protocol is made possible by the Azure Files service. This implies that the same files can be read and written to by several virtual machines (VMs). The REST interface or the storage client libraries can also be used to access the files. You no longer have to host your own file share in an Azure virtual machine and deal with the complex setup needed to make it highly available thanks to the Files service.

This is applicable to numerous typical situations:

- File shares are used by many on-premises apps, which facilitates the migration of data-sharing apps to Azure.

140

- Multiple virtual machines can access configuration files that are kept on a file share.

- It is possible to store diagnostic logs, metrics, crash dumps, etc. on a file share for processing and examined later.

- To guarantee that everyone in the group utilizes the same version and has access to them, tools and utilities that are utilized by several developers might be kept on a file share.

You can access the share using the drive letter or network URL that was assigned to it after mounting it like you would any other file share to make it visible to a virtual machine. The format of the network URL is \\[share name](dot)file(dot)core(dot)windows(dot)net\[storage account name]. Once the share has been mounted, you can add, modify, remove, and read the directories and files by using the regular file system APIs.

As of this writing, the Azure Files Preview is only visible in the Microsoft Azure Management Portal to verify that the feature is enabled; it is not visible at all in the Microsoft Azure Preview Portal. To accomplish this, access the storage account by logging into the Azure Management Portal. The

141

files.core.windows.net domain will be used to display the endpoint URL.

You need to utilize PowerShell, the REST APIs, one of the storage client libraries, or AzCopy, a Microsoft command-line tool, in order to build or view a file share or upload or download files to it from outside of Azure.

There are several restrictions because this is a preview feature:

- Only virtual machines (VMs) located in the same region as the storage account can access the share when using SMB 2.1. However, you can use the REST APIs to retrieve the data from any location.
- Azure Files are not supported by the storage emulation. Up to 5 TB of files may be shared.
- The maximum throughput per share is 60 MB/s.
- The files uploaded to the sharing have a 1 TB size limit. Each share may have up to 1,000 IOPS (of size 8 KB).
- Access control lists (ACLs) and Active Directory-based authentication are not supported at this time, however this is anticipated to change in the future.

142

Currently, access to the file share is authenticated using the Azure Storage account credentials. To optimize efficiency, it may be better to divide a collection of files among several shares if they are often visited.

STORAGE FOR TABLES

Large volumes of semistructured, nonrelational data can be stored with Azure Table Storage, a scalable NoSQL data store. It prevents you from executing stored procedures, using foreign keys, and performing sophisticated joins. To facilitate speedy data queries, each table has a single clustered index. Additionally, you can use OData with the WCF Data Service.NET libraries and LINQ queries to access the data. Table storage is frequently used for logging diagnostics.

You must first create a storage account in order to use table storage. You can make tables and add data to them if you have a storage account. A set of key/value pairs is contained in each of the entities (rows) that make up a table. Three system attributes are present in every entity: a timestamp, a partition key, and a row key. The partition key and row key combination, which together constitute the table's primary key, must be distinct. In order to provide load balancing among storage nodes, the rows are sharded (partitioned)

143

using the PartitionKey attribute. The same storage node houses all entities that have the same PartitionKey. Within a specified partition, uniqueness is provided by the RowKey.

You should carefully consider the PrimaryKey and RowKey as well as how you need to get the data in order to get the optimum performance. Scalability goals are offered by the Azure Table service for partitions and storage accounts. Azure is responsible for maintaining the Timestamp attribute, which shows the last modification date and time of the entity. This is how the Azure Table service supports optimistic concurrency with ETags.

Every entity has a set of key/value pairs known as properties in addition to the system properties. Since there is no schema, values of various properties may be included in key/value pairs. One entity can have the payload {customer id, customer name, request date/time, request} while logging using the Semantic Logging Application Block, for instance. The next entity might have {customer id, order id, item count, date-time order filled}. Each table object can hold up to 252 key/value pairs.

Up to a storage account's size restriction, the number of tables is infinite.

144

The storage client library can be used to manage tables. A REST API that implements the OData protocol is also supported by the Table service; tables can be addressed using the OData protocol by a URL in the style http://[storage account name]/table.core.windows.net/[table name]

QUEUES

Messages are stored and retrieved using the Azure Queue service. Millions of messages can be stored in a queue, up to the storage account's maximum limit, and queue messages can have a maximum size of 64 KB.

Generally speaking, queues are used to compile a list of messages for asynchronous processing. Best-effort first-in, first-out (FIFO) queues are supported by the Queue service. You may, for instance, have a worker role that continuously scans a queue for messages. Once it locates a message, it processes it before taking it out of the queue. The processing of images is among the most prevalent examples.

Assume you have a web application that enables users to upload pictures to a blob storage container. Each image must have a thumbnail created by your program. You place a message with the customer ID and container name on a queue instead of making the customer wait while this processing is completed. A worker role then retrieves the message and parses it to obtain the container name and customer ID. After retrieving each image, the worker role makes a thumbnail and saves it to the same blob storage bucket as the original. The worker role deletes the message from the queue once every image has been processed. What happens if you need to store more than 64 KB of data in the message? You could then write a file containing the data to a blob in blob storage and include the file's URL in the queue message. After retrieving the message from the queue, the worker role might use the URL to read the file from blob storage and do the necessary processing. You should be mindful of each message's Invisibility Timeout attribute. You must delete a message from a queue after using it; retrieving a message from a queue does not remove it from the queue. The message is rendered invisible upon being read from the queue. If the message is not removed from the queue within the allotted period, it becomes visible for processing once more. This is known as the Invisibility Timeout.

Generally speaking, you want to set this property to the maximum amount of time required to process a message. This way, while one worker role instance is processing the message, another instance of the same role does not see it (visible) in the queue and attempts to process it

146

simultaneously. In any case, it is essential that all message processing be idempotent, meaning that no matter how frequently the message is processed—even if it is done simultaneously—the same result should be obtained. Reading the message from the queue, deleting it, and then beginning to process it is not what you want to do. That queue entry won't ever be processed if the worker role instance goes offline. The case of the worker role instance shutting down is handled by leaving the message on the queue (but invisible) until the processing is finished; eventually, the message will be visible again and processed by another instance of the worker role.

Using a separate queue for every step allows you to mimic a workflow. It is possible to process a message from one queue, remove it when finished, and then start processing for the subsequent step in the workflow by placing a new message on a different queue.

The **dequeue count** is used by the Queue service to support poison messages. The issue is that if an invalid message is handled by an application, it may crash, making the message visible in the queue once more and crashing the application that processes it next. A message like that is

147

105

They call it a toxic message. By looking at the message's dequeue count, you can avoid this. If this goes above a certain point, the message should be removed from the queue, its processing halted, and a copy placed in a different poison message queue for offline examination. You may either manually examine those entries as they accumulate or process them on a regular basis and send an email whenever an entry is added to the queue.

You can obtain up to 32 messages in a single call and process each one separately if you choose to process the queue messages in batches.

REDUNDANCY

What occurs if the storage node that houses your blobs malfunctions? What occurs if the storage node's rack malfunctions? Thankfully, Azure has a feature called replication. When you create the storage account, you choose which of the four replication types to utilize. With the exception of Zone Redundant Storage, replication parameters can be altered once they are established. Azure Storage's Locally Redundant Storage (LRS) ensures high availability by making three synchronous copies of all

148

data before a write is considered successful. These copies are kept in one location inside one area. The replicas are located in different upgrade and fault domains. This implies that even in the event that a storage node that houses your data malfunctions or is taken offline for updating, the data will still be accessible.

Azure sends a request to update storage to each of the three replicas and waits for each to answer successfully before getting back to you. This indicates that the primary datacenter's copies are constantly in sync.

It is advised that you avoid using this for production data, which needs continuous access, as your data will be unavailable if the entire datacenter has an outage. GRS stands for Geo-Redundant Storage. For high availability, GRS creates three synchronous LRS copies of the data in the primary region. For disaster recovery, it creates three asynchronous LRS replicas in a paired area. For GRS, every Azure region has a matched region that is specified inside the same geographical border. For instance, the East and West US are paired. The storage account's scalability goals are marginally impacted by this. GRS is best considered as catastrophe recovery for Microsoft, not for you, and you cannot access the GRS copies in the paired

149

region. Microsoft would make the GRS clones available in the event of a significant failure in the primary area, but this has never occurred.

GEO-REDUNDANT READ-ACCESS STORAGE (RA-GRS)

It is appropriate for customer disaster recovery since it combines GRS with the capability to read data in the secondary area. You can modify your application to have read-only access to the paired area in the event that the primary region is problematic. Even if your clients might not be able to update, the data remains accessible for reporting, viewing, etc.

This can also be applied to applications where a large number of users view the data but only a small number of users can write to it. The paired region can be accessed by those who are merely reading the data, while your program that writes the data can be directed to the primary region. When accessing a storage account, this is an excellent approach to spread out the performance.

Only block blobs can use the new Zone Redundant Storage (ZRS) option. Within a single region or between two regions, it duplicates your data between two to three facilities.

150

Compared to LRS, this offers more longevity; nevertheless, ZRS accounts lack logging and monitoring features.

ESTABLISHING AND OVERSEEING STORAGE

We create a storage account and examine the available options in this part. Additionally, we establish a container in Blob Storage and demonstrate how to use Visual Studio to upload some blobs into the container. Next, we use Visual Studio's Server Explorer to construct a table and demonstrate how to add some records to it.

HOW TO MAKE A STORAGE ACCOUNT

- Go to the Azure Preview Portal (portal.azure.com) to create a storage account.
- In the lower-left corner, click +NEW.
- Then choose Storage.
- You must first give the storage account a name.
- In the endpoints for blobs, files, tables, and queues, this will be the name of the storage account.
- The PRICING TIER is the following field. You should see something like the image below.

151

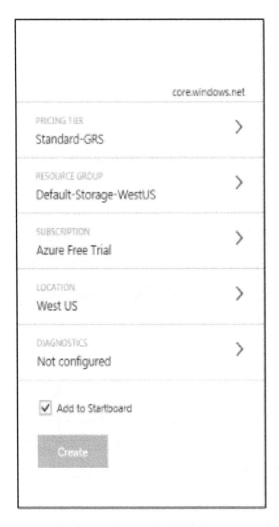

- L1 is Locally Redundant Storage (LRS), R1 is Read-Access Geo-Redundant Storage (RA-GRS), and G1 is Geo-Redundant Storage (GRS). Zone Redundant Storage (ZRA) will be displayed as an option along

152

with additional details about each tier if you click
BROWSE ALL PRICING TIERS at the bottom of
this window. The price per 100 GB per month is also

153

displayed on the detail screen. Because this is for testing and development and not production, choose Locally Redundant Storage (LRS).

- Then click Select at the bottom of the screen.

The **RESOURCE GROUP** field, which is used to manage a group of resources or assets, comes next. For instance, you would place both of them in the same resource group if you were only going to use this storage account with a particular website. This enables you to jointly administer such resources. That is not what we will do right now. By selecting RESOURCE GROUP, you can either choose an existing group that has been created for you or create a new one.

There are resource groups for the websites, storage accounts, and cloud services that have been created in the Azure Management Portal as part of this subscription.

- Choose Create A New Resource Group
- Enter a name, and click OK at the bottom of the Create Resource Group blade since we don't want this storage account linked to any other resources.
- The subscription of the current account that is currently logged into the portal is then shown.

154

- Clicking SUBSCRIPTION will display the other accounts if you are the administrator of multiple subscriptions using the same Microsoft account.
- From there, you can choose which account you want this storage account linked to.

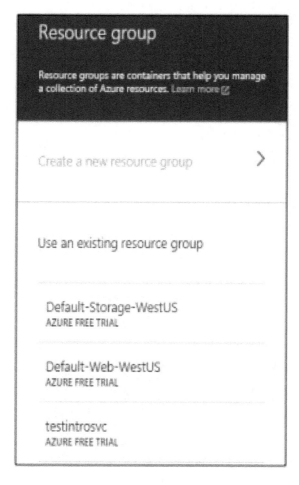

- **LOCATION** comes next. The location of the storage account will be in this area.

- Choose the one closest to your application, ensuring the lowest possible latency.

- The **diagnostics** come next. Clicking it will bring up the STATUS on the next screen.

- This toggle is used to get storage account analytics. When you write the data to the storage account, you will be charged for storage transactions.

- Click OK at the blade's bottom to activate the diagnostics.

- Click Create at the bottom of the Add Storage Account screen after checking the Add To Startboard box. Your storage account will be provisioned by Azure and added to your Startboard for easy access.

- A blade containing all of your storage account's details will appear if you click on your new storage account from the Startboard.

You may view details about your storage account, including the Blob, Queue, and Table service endpoints, by selecting **PROPERTIES**. If you need to modify the access keys, you can regenerate them or retrieve them by clicking **KEYS**. The storage account will be accessed using one of the keys and the name of the storage account.

156

This blade has additional parts for usage and monitoring. To utilize these capabilities, Diagnostics must be activated. Azure will continue to use a set of default metrics. You can also choose the retention period and other metrics. The default metrics for Azure include the total egress for blobs, tables, and queues because you pay for egress but not for ingress. In order to be informed if any of your alert rules are activated, you can also set up alerts for any of the metrics. The Azure Preview Portal does not currently offer the ability to set up a custom domain.

Nevertheless, you can log in straight to manage(dot)windowsazure(dot)com or click a button to access the Azure Management Portal.

HOW TO MAKE A CONTAINER AND PUT BLOBS IN IT

Let's construct a container in our new storage account and upload some files to it now that we have a new storage account.

- Click on the new storage account you added to your Startboard after logging into the Azure Preview Portal (portal(dot)azure(dot)com).
- Next, under the SUMMARY section, click CONTAINERS.

157

- There aren't any containers because the storage account was freshly created.
- Press ADD+. As seen above you will be asked for the access type and the container name.
- Who can access the container and the blobs is determined by the Access Type.
- If this is set to Private, only those with the account credentials (account name and key) or a URL that contains a security token will be able to access the container and the blobs within it. Setting this to Blob will allow anybody with a URL to read the associated blob, but not the container's metadata, properties, or list of blobs.
- Everyone gets read access to the container and its contents if this is set to Container.
- To add the container, select Blob and click OK at the bottom of the screen.

158

Keep in mind that the container name is part of the URL.

- The URL to every blob in the container will be this, concatenated with the blob name. Let's add some blobs now.
- When you click on the container, the message "This Container Has No Blobs" will appear.

Add a container

NAME

| |

Access type

Private
No anonymous access

Blob
Access blobs via anonymous requests

Container
List and access blobs via anonymous requests

159

HOW TO USE VISUAL STUDIO'S SERVER EXPLORER TO UPLOAD BLOBS

Additionally, you can use **Visual Studio's Server Explorer** to upload blobs. The name and key of the storage account are needed for this.

- As mentioned before, you can click on your storage account on the Startboard after logging into the Azure Preview Portal.

-

- After that, select KEYS from the SUMMARY section and copy one of the keys to the Windows

Clipboard.

- Click on the Server Explorer in Visual Studio.

- Choose Storage under Windows Azure. If you are asked for your Microsoft account information, enter it.

- Right-click Storage in the Server Explorer > WindowsAzure area, then choose Attach External Storage. The credentials for the storage account will be requested from you.

- Paste the account key in after entering the name of the storage account you added in the previous phase.

- To add the storage account, click OK. The storage account has now been added to Server Explorer's Storage branch.

- The files container that was previously inserted is visible.

HOW TO OPEN THE CONTAINER IN A DIFFERENT WINDOW

- To open the container in a different window, double-click on it.

- By clicking the button with the up arrow, you may now upload blobs.

- You can choose one or more files to be uploaded and click OK in the typical Windows File Explorer dialog box that appears.

- If the upload was successful, it will be shown in the Windows Azure Activity Log pane. Once many files have been uploaded

- Blobs can also be deleted, opened, and downloaded using Server Explorer.

- By right-clicking on Blobs and choosing Create Blob Container, you can even add containers.

This implementation of blob storage access is rather straightforward. You are unable to upload or download image-rich folders.

HOW TO MAKE A TABLE AND INCLUDE THE RECORDS

Let's add some entities to a table that we construct in our storage account. One of the storage explorer tools listed in the previous section can be used, but let's see how simple it is to complete this work using Visual Studio.

- This will be equally simple if you followed the instructions in the previous section to add blobs to blob storage.

-

163

- Open Visual Studio > Server Explorer and add the desired external storage account if you haven't

164

already.

- Right-click Tables in Server Explorer, then choose Create Table.

- The table's name, which must be distinct within your storage account, will be asked for.

- Double-click the table name after selecting OK to create the new table.

- By typing a WCF Data Services filter in the text box and clicking the green triangle to apply it, you can filter the view when using this feature to open a table containing numerous entities.

- Since we don't have any entities, let's add some by selecting the plus icon.

- To obtain the best performance, you need to consider what you want to use for PartitionKey and RowKey.

- Let's use the city name for the RowKey and the state abbreviation for the PartitionKey in this example. Add LandArea as a Double and Population as Int32 for properties. Complete each field with the appropriate values.

- Before the entity is added to the table, to save the entity, click OK.

- Add another entity, and this time, include a property like GPSCoordinates in addition to Population and

165

LandArea. Include a few more entities with whichever characteristics you desire.

- After saving an entity, you can right-click on it and choose Edit if you wish to make changes.
- This view can also be used to delete entities.
- After adding entities, view the table.

Here, each entity has a distinct PartitionKey and RowKey combination. The list of key/value pairs takes up the remainder of each table row. Not every entity has the same characteristics. Only LandArea and Population are available for the San Francisco entity, whereas GPSCoordinates are only available for the San Jose entity. Azure Tables' ability to allow key/value pairs to differ for every object is one of its advantages.

Tables can be created in Visual Studio using a designer like this one, but you will most likely need to write your own code using the storage client library to add, modify, and remove things.

VIRTUAL NETWORKS IN AZURE

Azure uses virtual networks, or VNets, to give your services an extra degree of protection and isolation. Services and virtual machines (VMs) connected to the same virtual network can communicate with one another. Services

166

outside the virtual network are by default unable to connect to services inside the network. However, you can set up the network so that the external service can be accessed. You get improved performance because services that communicate with one another within a virtual network do not pass through the Azure Load Balancer. Although it isn't important, sometimes every little bit matters.

This is an illustration of a situation in which a virtual network might be useful. Suppose you have a back-end database operating on a virtual machine and a front-end web application running in a cloud service. The web application will access the database through the virtual network if the back-end database is located in the same virtual network as the cloud service. This enables you to access the cloud service's back-end database without having to worry about it being publicly available online.

A virtual network in Azure can be made an extension of your on-premises network by adding a Virtual Network Gateway to it and using it to link your on-premises network to Azure. Deploying hybrid cloud apps that safely link to your on-premises datacenter is made possible by this. One of Azure's fully managed services is the Virtual Network Gateway. Multisite VPNs, in-region VNet-to-VNet, and cross-region

167

VNet-to-VNet are among the more sophisticated features that are available. The majority of cross-premises connections require establishing a secure connection to your Azure virtual network using a VPN device. VNet-to-VNet communication connects two or more virtual networks over IPsec/IKE S2S VPN tunnels via the Azure Virtual Network Gateway. When integrating one or more on-premises locations with your virtual networks, this offers you flexibility. You can have cross-region geo-redundancy, like SQL Always On across many Azure regions.

The address space, subnets, and DNS servers you wish to utilize are some of the things you need to know while building a virtual network.

ADDRESS SPACES FOR VIRTUAL NETWORKS

Setting up a virtual network involves defining its topology, which includes the subnets and address spaces that are available. Address ranges that do not overlap should be used if the virtual network is to be connected to other virtual networks. Your network's virtual machines and services are allowed to use this range of addresses. These are private and inaccessible from the public Internet, thus you need to utilize unroutable IP addresses, like 10.0.0.0/8, 172.16.0.0/12, or 192.168.0.0/16, which are listed in CIDR notation.

Unroutable IP addresses are only used on internal networks; they cannot receive traffic on the public Internet. By combining an IP address with the network mask that goes with it, CIDR defines an address range. Since n is the number of leftmost '1' bits in the mask, CIDR notation takes the following format: xxx.xxx.xxx.xxx/n. For instance, 192.168.12.0/23 starts at 192.168.12.0 and applies the network mask 255.255.254.0 to the 192.168 network. Thus, the address range 192.168.12.0–192.168.13.255 is represented by this notation.

Thankfully, the Azure Management Portal shows this information in a drop-down list, saving you from having to calculate it bit by bit! Your usable address range is 10.0.0.0– 10.255.255.255 if you choose 10.0.0.0/8. You can definitely utilize this, but you want to make sure there isn't any overlap if 10.0.0.0 is being used elsewhere in the network, whether on-premises or in Azure.

Choosing a smaller address space that can still accommodate all you wish to put in it is one method to accomplish this. For instance, you may select 10.0.0.0/27, which provides you with a useful address range of 10.0.0.0–10.0.0.31, if you are only planning to add a few virtual machines to your virtual network.

169

If you are employed by a company where someone else is in charge of the internal networks, you should speak with them before choosing your address space to ensure that there is no overlap and to inform them of your preference so they won't try to use the same range of IP addresses.

SUBNETS

You can construct one or more subnets for your virtual network after defining your address space or spaces. By doing this, you divide your network into smaller, easier-to-manage segments. For instance, you may designate VMs with 10.1.0.0, back-end cloud services with 10.2.0.0, and SQL Server VMs with 10.3.0.0.

Keep in mind that Azure keeps each subnet's initial four addresses for its own purposes. Because there isn't a security boundary between subnets by default, services in each subnet can communicate with each other. The ability to create Network Security Groups, which are linked to sets of allow and deny rules for the Internet, the virtual network, or IP ranges (represented in CIDR form), was recently disclosed by Microsoft. Subnets can then be linked to each Network Security Group or VM, enabling the establishment of VM and subnet ACLs to regulate the network traffic permitted to and from VMs and subnets.

Traffic is divided by broadcast domain when subnets are used, and routing is necessary to transfer traffic to another subnet. This helps keep chatty traffic from interfering with other network traffic. To prevent things like big downloads from interfering with phone traffic, many firms, for instance, conduct their VoIP traffic on a separate subnet from their desktops.

DNS SERVERS

A DNS service is required to perform name resolution if you wish to refer to your virtual machines (VMs) or role instances by host name or fully qualified domain name (FQDN) directly instead of utilizing an IP address and port number. Determining this prior to the deployment of virtual machines or role instances is beneficial. Because the DNS server information is put into the settings at launch, changing it later will require rebooting every virtual machine in the virtual network.

You have two choices:

- You can utilize the name resolution offered by Azure,

Or

- You can designate a DNS server that is not managed by Azure, like the one your on-premises

171

infrastructure uses or that you install and manage in an Azure virtual machine.

You must use your own DNS server if you require name resolution across cloud services. For instance, you will require your own DNS server solution if you have two virtual machines (VMs) on the same virtual network and you want them to be able to interact by host name. You can add a virtual machine (VM) running DNS to your virtual network if you don't want to use any on-premises DNS servers.

HOW TO ESTABLISH A VIRTUAL NETWORK

To add virtual machines (VMs) to a virtual network, first construct the virtual network and then assign each VM to the virtual network and subnet. During deployment, virtual machines and cloud services pick up their network configurations.

When virtual machines are installed, they are given an IP address. Multiple virtual machines (VMs) are issued IP addresses during bootup if they are deployed into a virtual network or subnet. The internal IP address linked to a virtual machine is called a DIP. A static DIP can be assigned to a role instance or virtual machine. In order to prevent unintentionally reusing a static DIP for another virtual

172

machine, you might think about utilizing a distinct subnet for static DIPs.

It is not an easy configuration adjustment to convert a virtual machine (VM) into a virtual network. The virtual machines must be redeployed into the virtual network. The simplest method is to remove the virtual machine (VM) but leave all of its disks intact, then use the original disks in the virtual network to recreate the VM. All you have to do is add a cloud service (web roles and worker roles) to a virtual network.

Information about the virtual network is displayed in the Network Configuration Section of the Service Configuration file. The cloud service will be installed in the virtual network upon deployment.

HOW TO BUILD VIRTUAL NETWORK USING THE QUICK CREATE OPTION

Let's try building a virtual network using the Quick Create option.

- Go to manage(dot)windowsazure(dot)com, the Azure Management Portal, and log in.
- Select NETWORK SERVICES > VIRTUAL NETWORK > QUICK CREATE
- After clicking the +NEW button at the bottom of the screen. You ought to notice something like this:

173

Jason Taylor

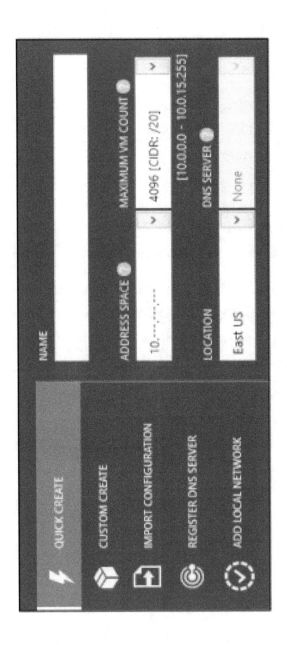

174

- Enter the NAME you would like to use for your network.
- After that, pick your ADDRESS SPACE.
- As was previously mentioned, there are only three options available in the drop-down list: These are 192.168.0.0, 172.16.0.0, and 10.0.0.0.
- Choose 10.---------.---.
- The range of IP addresses included for the chosen CIDR is known as the MAXIMUM VM COUNT. The greatest CIDR (and hence the fewest amount of IP addresses) is 20, which provides you with 4,096 addresses, if you examine the figures in the drop-down list.
- Choose the preferred area for LOCATION.
- If you leave DNS SERVER set to None, Azure will handle name resolution.
- You should specify the DNS servers you use for your on-premises name resolution if you wish to have name resolution between this virtual network and your on-premises network. Simply set it to None for this example.
- At the bottom of the screen, select the CREATE A VIRTUAL NETWORK checkmark.
- Your virtual network will now be provided by Azure.

175

- After it is complete, you will have a virtual network that you can use to set up your services and virtual machines.

PERSONALIZED CREATION

Let's now examine the choices that might be used when creating a virtual network using Custom Create.

- Choose +NEW > NETWORK SERVICES > VIRTUAL NETWORK > CUSTOM CREATE from the Azure Management Portal. You ought to notice something like this:

176

- Click the arrow in the bottom-right corner of the screen after entering a unique NAME and selecting the appropriate LOCATION.

- To utilize Azure's name resolution, leave the DNS SERVERS boxes empty on the following page.

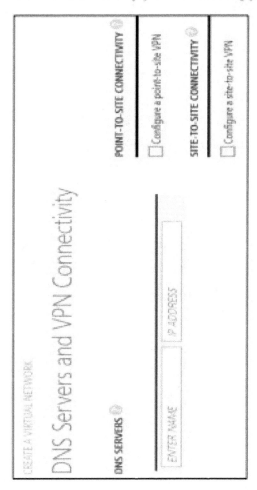

177

- At this stage, you would indicate that you wish to set up a site-to-site or point-to-site VPN. Later in this chapter, we'll look at how to set up a point-to-site network.

- To proceed to the following page, click the right arrow at the bottom of the screen and leave these check boxes unchecked for the time being.

- The address space(s) and subnets for each can be specified here.

- The typical suspects can be found if you examine the values in the STARTING IP drop-down list: These are 192.168.0.0, 172.16.0.0, and 10.0.0.0.

- Choose 10.0.0.0. 5. The CIDR can then be specified. The address range of 10.0.0.0 to 10.0.15.255 is provided by selecting /20.

- A subnet for 10.0.0.0 through 10.0.0.255 and another for 10.0.1.0 through 10.0.1.255 will be configured.

- To modify this name to something more meaningful, click Subnet-1. Change the CIDR to 24 but keep the STARTING IP at 10.0.0.0. The range 10.0.0.0 to 10.0.0.255 will be yours as a result.

- After that, select Add Subnet to add an editable entry. Set the CIDR to /24, the name, and the first IP

178

address to 10.0.1.0. The range 10.0.1.0 to 10.0.1.255 will be yours as a result.

- We don't need to add extra address spaces, but you are welcome to do so. You need to see something like this screen after completing the fields: To establish the network, click the checkmark in the bottom-right corner of the screen.

- Two subnets are now part of your virtual network. In the aforementioned scenario, we would set up data services (such SQL Server virtual machines) in MyDataSvcs and virtual machines and PaaS instances on the MyVMs subnet.

HOW TO UTILIZE A FILE FOR NETWORK CONFIGURATION

Uploading a network configuration file is an additional method of configuring a virtual network. Making one of these from scratch is challenging; the simplest method is to retrieve the existing network configuration file, make changes, and then upload it once more. The full subscription is covered by the network configuration file.

If you have a subscription that includes virtual networks and you wish to clone one or more of them to another subscription, this capability can be useful.

The network configuration file can be exported. The network configuration file should be exported. This creates an XML file that contains the complete Azure subscription.

- Click NETWORKS in the left column of the Azure Management Portal

(manage(dot)windowsazure(dot)com).

- This will display the networks that you have configured.
- At the bottom of the screen, select EXPORT. A subscription prompt will appear. It will display a drop-down list if you are the administrator of several subscriptions.
- Click the checkmark at the bottom of the screen after selecting the subscription for which you want to export the network configuration file.

CHAPTER SIX

HOW TO UPLOAD FILE TO A SUBSCRIPTION THAT DOESN'T USE VIRTUAL NETWORKS

Let's upload file to a subscription that doesn't use virtual networks. It ought to produce the same collection of virtual networks. To ensure that new virtual networks are formed, remove the two that we made before importing this file if you don't already have another Azure membership.

- Go to manage(dot)windowsazure(dot)com, the Azure Management Portal. Click +NEW > Network Services > Virtual Network > Import Configuration in the bottom-left corner.

- A popup to search for the network configuration file will appear.

- Click the arrow at the bottom of the screen after searching for it. It demonstrates what it will do today. It claims that it will produce both of them because I'm utilizing a second membership.

- At the bottom of the screen, click the checkmark. These two virtual networks will now be provisioned into the subscription by Azure with the same address spaces and subnets.

181

WHAT-IF SCENARIOS

Many questions are raised by this since you are unable to download only the configuration for one of the virtual networks specified in the subscription; instead, you must download the entire subscription configuration:

- Is it possible to change one of the virtual networks' settings?
- Is it possible to add an additional virtual network?
- Is it possible to eliminate a few of the virtual networks?
- What happens if services or virtual machines are already set up in the virtual network?

Let's examine how Azure responds to a few scenarios.

Azure looks for discrepancies when you upload the network configuration file. It notifies you before making the adjustment if any are discovered.

What if a network is added?

You will see it if you add a network to the configuration file without altering the existing networks. Before Azure commits the change, you must approve it.

What happens if a network is eliminated?

182

Azure will detect when a network is removed from the configuration and ask for your approval.

The dialog box will appear if you attempt to remove a section that contains virtual machines (VMs) or other services deployed into it. However, an error message stating that the network configuration file could not be imported will appear when you attempt to commit the changes.

What happens if you switch networks?

Azure will display the dialog box if you make changes to the configuration for a network that does not yet have any virtual machines or services installed on it.

This dialog box will still appear if you attempt to modify a network that has virtual machines (VMs) or other services installed on it, but Azure will indicate that the network configuration file could not be imported when you attempt to commit the changes.

The changes (whether they be additions, revisions, or deletions) will be applied if you upload a network configuration file containing changes to a network without anything being deployed into it. Your changes will be refused if you upload a network configuration file with

183

modifications to a network that has anything deployed on it (such a virtual machine or cloud service).

OPTIONS FOR CROSS-PREMISES CONNECTIONS

There are numerous situations when you may wish to connect to your Azure infrastructure from your home network, a customer's site, your on-premises network, or even a coffee shop while maintaining security. Site-to-site VPN, point-to-site VPN, and private VPN (ExpressRoute) are the three options that Azure offers to assist you in setting up these cross-premises connections.

In order to link point-to-site and site-to-site, you need to configure a VPN gateway in Azure. This gateway serves as the point of entry into Azure from either the client computer (point-to-site) or the on-premises network (site-to-site). Later in this chapter, when we build up a point-to-site network, you'll see how to accomplish this. Connectivity between sites

You can safely link your on-premises network to your Azure virtual network using a site-to-site VPN. An IPv4 IP address that is visible to the public and a VPN or Routing and Remote Access (RRAS) device that is compatible with Windows Server are prerequisites. Computers and virtual machines (VMs) on your local network can communicate with the resources in the Azure virtual network after the connection is established. For instance, if you host a business application on Azure, your staff can use your site-to-site network to safely access and run that application. In fact, you may link whole on-premises networks to Azure virtual networks using site-to-site connection. A business that has several branch offices is a good example. It is possible to link Azure to the network of each branch office.

POINT-TO-SITE COMMUNICATION

POINT-TO-SITE WITH A VPN

you can connect to your Azure virtual network from your local computer over a Secure Socket Tunneling Protocol (SSTP) tunnel. This makes use of certificate authentication between the Azure virtual network and the client computer. This implies that you must generate a few certificates and install them appropriately.

NETWORK POINT-TO-SITE

It is advised that you make a distinct client certificate for every client that will connect to the point-to-site network and maintain a record of the thumbnail of the certificate and the computer that installed it. You can use the Azure subscription ID, the virtual network name, and the certificate thumbprint to invalidate the client certificate if you need to later disable

185

access for a single user. The only option to revoke access if you use the same client certificate on several machines is to delete the root certificate in Azure. This will remove access for all client certificates that chain back to that root certificate.

Up to 128 customers can be connected to Azure's virtual network. (Each gateway has a maximum bandwidth of 80 MBPS.) Every client computer you wish to utilize must have the connection set up. Although you can set up the VPN to start automatically, if necessary, once it is configured, the user can start the VPN by manually opening the connection.

COMPARING CONNECTION BETWEEN SITES AND POINTS

These two types of secure communications differ in a number of ways:

- To use a point-to-site network, you do not require an RRAS or a VPN equipment.
- Every client computer needs to be configured when using point-to-site. The client computers don't need to be altered while using site-to-site.
- Point-to-site works well in situations where: Only a small number of your clients require access. A VPN

186

device that you can use for a site-to-site connection is not available to you.

- When offsite, whether at a customer site or coffee shop, you want to connect securely. Both site-to-site and point-to-site networks can operate concurrently.

- If you are able to set up a site-to-site network, you may use it for individuals who are on-site and permit point-to-site for those who must join from a distance.

PRIVATE SITE-TO-SITE CONNECTIVITY (EXPRESSROUTE)

Not to be overlooked is private site-to-site connectivity, which is represented by ExpressRoute in Azure. This is referred regarded as private because, unlike site-to-site and point-to-site connectivity, network traffic passes through your network provider rather than the public Internet. This feature guarantees that Azure may be used to design and execute applications with privacy needs. Additionally, using ExpressRoute increases speed, dependability, and reduces latency.

Either hardware collocated at an Exchange provider (such Equinix or Level 3) or an extra site on your MPLS VPN-based WAN via a network server provider is how the network connects on your end with this choice. Azure is directly connected to via the network service provider or Exchange provider. Multiple virtual networks within the same Azure geography (continent) can be connected to via a single ExpressRoute circuit.

Azure offers free inbound bandwidth at all times. If you use ExpressRoute with a network service provider, you can send and receive a limitless amount of data. You get a lot of bandwidth when you use an Exchange provider. As a result, ExpressRoute can drastically reduce the cost of data transfers if you have workloads that include large volumes of data leaving the Azure datacenter. The bandwidth can vary from 10 MBPS to 10 GPBS, depending on the provider you choose.

When it comes to providing enterprise-grade solutions, this is the finest option. Applications or workloads that are mission vital to your business are a suitable fit for it. ExpressRoute is a fantastic option if you have SLAs in place with groups inside or outside of your company because of its reliable network performance.

NETWORK POINT-TO-SITE

This section demonstrates how to deploy a virtual machine (VM) into the network and connect to it from the local PC in order to set up and test a point-to-site network. An outline of the setup procedure. These are the procedures we will use to set up a point-to-site network that we can access from our local computer.

- Establish a virtual network and allow point-to-site communication.
- Set up a virtual machine on the network.
- Establish a gateway for the network.
- Produce a root certificate that is self-signed.
- Using the root certificate, generate a self-signed client certificate.
- From the certificate store, export the client certificate.
- Provide Azure with the root authentication certificate.
- To authenticate to the virtual network, install the client certificate on the client computer.
- Set up the VPN client software.
- Create the VPN connection and confirm it.

HOW TO SET UP A VPN POINT-TO-SITE
- Enter the Azure Management Portal (manage(dot)windowsazure(dot)com) to get started.

189

- In this demonstration, we set up the gateway for point-to-site connectivity after creating the virtual network and deploying a virtual machine (VM) into it.

HOW TO ESTABLISH A VIRTUAL NETWORK

190

- Select +NEW > VIRTUAL NETWORK > NETWORK SERVICES > CUSTOM CREATE.

This brings up the screen that is displayed here:

- Click the right arrow at the bottom of the screen after choosing the desired LOCATION and entering the NAME.
- ContosoP2S for NAME and West US for LOCATION will be used in this example.
- To set up a point-to-site VPN, use the Configure A Point-To-Site VPN check box on the DNS Servers And VPN Connectivity page and accept the default settings.
- To proceed, click the right arrow.
- Choose the IP address range from which your VPN customers will get their IP addresses upon connection on the next screen. Let's use 10.0.0.0/24 as the default.
- To proceed, click the right arrow.

Next, we configure the address space that our virtual network will use:

- Let's start with IP 10.0.18.0 and a /24 CIDR. This provides us with the 10.0.18.0 to 10.0.18.255 address range.

- Use CIDR 27 and rename the subnet to P2SVMs.

- A gateway subnet must be included here if we wish to use a point-to-site network. By selecting Add Gateway Subnet, 10.0.18.32/29 will be added by default.

- Click the checkmark in the lower-right corner of the screen to accept the default and move on to the next screen. You can then deploy a virtual machine (VM) into the network after Azure has finished creating the virtual network.

HOW TO INSTALL A VIRTUAL MACHINE ON THE NETWORK

We will use the Azure Management Portal to create our virtual machine (VM) because the remainder of this chapter makes use of it.

- Click +NEW > COMPUTE > VIRTUAL MACHINE > FROM GALLERY to begin deploying a virtual machine (VM) onto the virtual network.

- After choosing Windows Server R2 Datacenter, click the bottom right arrow.

192

- Enter the VM name and then the user name and password on the Virtual Machine Configuration page. This account is used to access the virtual machine (VM) through Remote Desktop (RDP). To get to the next page, click the right arrow.

- Enter a distinct cloud service DNS name on the second setting screen.

- Choose the virtual network you established in this part from the drop-down list labeled REGION/AFFINITY GROUP/VIRTUAL NETWORK.

- Choose the required subnet from the drop-down list of VIRTUAL NETWORK SUBNETS. You can either choose an existing storage account that you have created in the same area or have Azure create a new one for you.

- To proceed, click the right arrow at the bottom of the screen.

- Click the checkmark in the lower-right corner of the screen and simply accept the settings on the last screen.

- Your virtual machine will now be provisioned and started in your virtual network by Azure.

193

- We can return to our network and finish building the network gateway while this is going on.

HOW TO CONSTRUCT THE VPN GATEWAY

- At the top of the screen, select the DASHBOARD tab. It will inform you that the gateway is still in the process of being constructed.
- At the bottom of the screen, click the +GATEWAY button.
- Click YES when prompted to create a gateway for your virtual network. Azure is currently building your point-to-site connectivity gateway.
- This will take a few minutes, so while it works, you can continue working on the certificate chores. Make a certificate of authentication for your virtual network.

As described earlier, you need to establish a self-signed root certificate and a client certificate for authentication when connecting to the VM on the network from the client. This is because point-to-site communication employs certificate authentication instead of password authentication, which is relatively weak. Even if someone manages to get the network's IP address, they will not be able to join to the virtual network if they do not have the right client certificate

194

installed. These are the procedures we use to create the certificates.

- Create a root certificate that is self-signed.
- Upload the root certificate to the Azure Management Portal.
- Generate a client certificate that uses the root certificate you just created.
- Export and install the client certificate on the client machine that is going to join to the network.
- The makecert.exe file is required in order to generate certificates. This should be installed if you have Visual Studio installed in any version.

The quickest method to locate it is to launch a command prompt window, navigate to the C drive's root, and use the following command to look for it: Makecert.exe dir/s

Installing Visual Studio Express will include it in the installation if you are unable to locate it. Move makecert.exe to a location that is convenient to access in the command window, like C:\makecert\. Then, open a command window and type cd C:\makecert to access that directory. You can now start creating your certificates.

- Make a root certificate that is self-signed.

Jason Taylor

- Using the root certificate you just made, produce a self-signed client certificate.

196

- The client certificate is created and installed on the local computer as a result. You must export the certificate, copy it to the other workstation, and import it in order to utilize it on other client computers.

- To save the client certificate to a file, locate the certificate in the certificate manager, then click Export. Open the run box (WindowsKey+R), type certmgr.msc, then hit Enter to launch the certificate manager.

- Select Personal, followed by Certificates. A list of certifications will appear on the right. Locate the ContosoP2SClient one that was issued by ContosoP2SRoot.

- Choose All Tasks > Export after performing a right-click on the ContosoP2SClient certificate. The Export dialog box opens as a result. Press Next.

- Click Next after choosing Yes to export the private key on the following screen.

- Click Next after accepting the Personal Information Exchange—PKCS #12 (.PFX) option by default and checking the box to include all certificates in the certification path if at all possible.

197

- Enter a password and the confirmation password after selecting the Password check box. Press Next.

- Enter the file name and path. ContosoP2SClient.pfx will be used in this demonstration. On the Certificate Export Wizard page, click Next after accepting the name by clicking Save.

- On the following screen, select "Finish." The client certificate will now be exported to the designated location. Shut down the command window and certificate manager.

- When a client computer is connected to the point-to-site network, all client certificates that chain back to that root certificate will be accepted. For every client connecting, Microsoft advises generating a unique client certificate.

- You risk invalidating that one client certificate if you do this and maintain track of them and later need to remove someone's access.

- Upload the root certificate that you have self-signed.

The root authentication certificate must then be uploaded to Azure. The authentication handshake with the client computer uses this.

198

- Go to manage.windowsazure.com, the Azure Management Portal.

- On the left, select NETWORKS. In this area, click the network you already built.

- At the top of the screen, select CERTIFICATES.

- At the bottom of the screen, select UPLOAD. You need to locate the root certificate, which was the initial certificate you made.

- ContosoP2SRoot.cer was the product of this exercise. To upload the certificate, locate it on the local computer, select it, and then click the checkmark.

- You can now see that the messages stating that you require a certificate and that you have no gateway have disappeared when you return to the DASHBOARD tab.

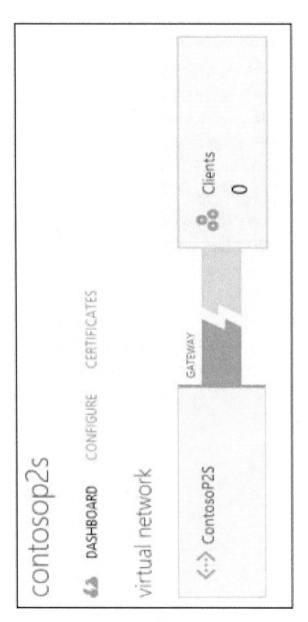

To authenticate the virtual network, install the client certificate (.pfx). For the virtual network handshake to be authenticated, the client computer has to have the certificate in its certificate store.

- Open the folder containing the client certificate file (in this case, it's ContosoP2SClient.pfx).
- To open the file, double-click on it. The Certificate Import Wizard will then open. As you proceed through the Certificate Import Wizard, accept all defaults and, when asked, input the password. When you previously exported the certificate, you set this password.
- Select Yes when asked to install the certificate. A dialog window stating that the import was successful ought to appear.
- Install the VPN client software.

Install the VPN software on the client computer after downloading it. By doing this, the virtual network will be added to the client computer's list of networks.

- Open the Azure Management Portal and find the DASHBOARD for your virtual network after logging into the client PC.

201

- There are two ways to download the client VPN package under Quick Glance on the right.

- Download the 64-bit or 32-bit package that corresponds to your computer. Instead of selecting Run when requested, select Save. This will have a file extension of .exe and a name that resembles a GUID.

- The file may be restricted to help safeguard your computer because it originated from an external place, particularly if you are using Windows 8 or later. Open Windows Explorer and navigate to the downloaded file to verify this and unblock it if necessary.

- When you right-click it, choose Properties. Click Unblock and then OK if it's blocked.

- Click the .exe file twice. Click "Yes" when asked to install the VPN client.

- Using the VPN client, connect to the virtual network.

Let's establish a connection to the virtual network from the client computer.

- To access your virtual network, click DASHBOARD in the Azure Management Portal.

- Locate the internal IP address of the virtual machine (VM) you previously created in this part (highlighted here) in the Resources section. When you RDP onto the network virtual machine, you will require this.

- On the right side of the taskbar, in the system tray, click the symbol for the Internet connection. Choose the virtual network from the list of connections that appears. The network in this case is called ContosoP2S.

- After selecting the virtual network, select Connect. The connection dialog box that follows appears:

203

- Press the Connect button. You will be asked to increase Connection Manager's privileges.
- To increase the privileges, click Continue. You can now RDP into the virtual machine (VM) after connecting to it via the virtual network.

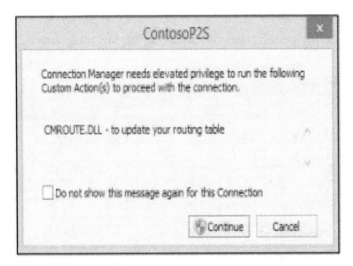

HOW TO USE THE INTERNAL IP ADDRESS TO CONNECT TO THE VIRTUAL MACHINE

Let's connect to the virtual machine (VM). We set up in the virtual network now that it's operational using RDP.

- Launch Remote Desktop first. You can choose it from the Start menu to accomplish this.

204

- Another option is to type mstsc, hit Enter, and then press WindowsKey+R.

- After retrieving the virtual machine's internal IP address from the Azure Management Portal, enter it in the computer text box and select Connect.

- Enter the login information you provided when you established the virtual machine. In the RDP warning dialog box, select Yes.

- This will allow you to access the virtual machine through the virtual network. Since you are connecting to the internal IP address, which is not accessible to the general public, you can be certain that you are using the virtual network.

- The network dashboard will now indicate that there is just one client connected (you may need to reload the page).

205

CHAPTER SEVEN
VERIFY THE VPN CONNECTION

Let's eliminate our virtual machine's public endpoints to ensure that the public cannot access it.

- Exit the virtual machine.
- Click VIRTUAL MACHINES on the left side of the Azure Management Portal, and then select the virtual machine (VM) located in the point-to-site network.
- At the top of the screen, select ENDPOINTS. At the bottom of the page, select DELETE after selecting the PowerShell endpoint.
- Click the Remote Desktop endpoint after it's done, then select DELETE at the bottom of the screen.
- You can still connect to the virtual machine by running RDP on the local computer. The point-to-site virtual network you created is being used.

DATABASES

Many applications rely on a persistent data storage. You will almost certainly need to communicate with a database as you develop new apps or move old ones to the Azure cloud. There are a number of alternatives available on the Azure platform. Relational database options like Azure SQL Database, SQL Server running in Azure Virtual Machines,

206

and non-Microsoft databases like Oracle or MySQL are all available to you. If your application requires a nonrelational, NoSQL database, services like DocumentDB and Azure Table Storage may be a good solution. Additionally, you can deploy a variety of database platforms using Azure Virtual Machines.

The Azure platform provides a range of database options when it comes to choosing a data storage strategy for your application, enabling you to strike a compromise between fully customized virtual machines and less hassle and control.

SQL DATABASE ON AZURE

A relational database-as-a-service, Azure SQL Database (previously known as SQL Azure) is designed to support workloads related to Online Transaction Processing (OLTP), or data entry and retrieval transactions. This clearly belongs to the PaaS cloud computing category. By choosing Azure SQL Database, you can keep the great majority of the administrative and logical management duties of a database server while relinquishing the physical administration duties. Elastic scale, predictable performance, business continuity, almost zero maintenance, and the utilization of well-known development languages and tools are just a few of the alluring benefits offered by Azure SQL Database.

207

It's critical to realize that Azure SQL Database does not provide you with a physically manageable server. Since Azure SQL Database is a database-as-a-service, you have no control over the specifics of its physical implementation. There are three levels of Azure SQL Database: Basic, Standard, and Premium. Database throughput units (DTUs) are used to express performance within these levels. A synthetic metric called a DTU makes it possible to compare the relative performance of different database tiers quickly. Performance levels (e.g., for Standard, S0, S1, and S2) also exist within each tier. The DTUs available within the tier can be changed using these performance levels. Each tier will have a different maximum database size, which can range from 2 GB to 500 GB.

Monitoring the performance of your application and then modifying Azure SQL Database tiers will typically determine which service tier to utilize. If necessary, you can advance from a Basic tier to a Standard or Premium tier. Since changing service tiers and performance levels is done online, you can keep using the database while the process is finished. There may be a brief drop in database connections when you are changing tiers and performance levels. To make your application resilient to such temporary problems, make sure to use retry logic.

The connection between a database and an Azure SQL Database server must be understood. A logical server is created when an Azure SQL Database server is created. The client and SQL Server, or in this case, Azure SQL Database, communicate via a Tabular Data Stream (TDS), which is basically what the logical Azure SQL Database server is (e.g., contoso.database.windows.net). There will be several instances of Azure SQL databases on that logical server.

The process of setting up a new Azure SQL Database server is incredibly fast. Using the Azure Preview Portal, construct a new Azure SQL Database server by selecting the featured list of new Azure services you can create by clicking the green **NEW** button located at the bottom left of the portal.

- To launch the blade and create a new SQL database, select the SQL Database option.

Several important pieces of data can be entered on the SQL Database blade:

- **Name**: Give the newly created database a name.
- **Pricing Tier**: Choose between the Basic, Standard, or Premium service tiers and the corresponding performance levels.

209

- **Collation**: Configure the collation used for data sorting and comparison rules.

- **The server**: Either build a new Azure SQL Database server or choose one that already exists. You can specify the Azure region, the administrative login credentials, and the server name (for example, contoso(dot)database(dot)windows(dot)net) when you create a new server.

- **Group of Resources**: Choose an already-existing logical group or establish a new one to house the Azure SQL database. Grouping relevant Azure resources together is made easier with resource groups.

- **Membership**: Choose the Azure subscription that you want.

- Click Create when you're done.

Azure may need several minutes to provision the new Azure SQL database. The new database will probably be available in a matter of seconds if you are building it on an already-existing server.

An Azure SQL Database instance can have a maximum size of 500 GB, as shown in Table 6-1 earlier in this chapter. You will need to employ a different approach to preserve the

210

required data if your data requirements are greater than what one database can hold. One such tactic is database sharding, which is the practice of distributing the data over several databases. Elastic scaling is made possible by the speed at which new database shards may be created. To enable an application to scale out across several databases, application owners can choose when and how to create additional database shards.

Azure SQL Database Elastic Scale is currently available in preview form.

MANAGEMENT

The almost low maintenance that Azure SQL Database offers is one of its alluring qualities. All database platform upgrades, load balancing, server configuration, and patching are automatically managed by Microsoft. Furthermore, Azure SQL Database automatically manages filegroups and system tables. Common administrative duties include maintaining the database's logical components, such as query optimization, index tuning, and login management.

The same tools, programming languages, and frameworks that you are accustomed to utilizing with a traditional SQL Server may be used with Azure SQL Database. Although not all SQL Server features are available in Azure SQL

211

Database, there are numerous similarities between the two databases (more on that later in this chapter). The two do, however, have one crucial thing in common: they both employ TDS as their client protocol. This makes it possible to connect to Azure SQL Database using tools like SQL Server Management Studio.

CONFIGURATION OF THE FIREWALL

You will probably need to change a firewall configuration before you can connect to Azure SQL Database from any tool, including SQL Server Management Studio. Firewall settings that specifically block access from any IP address, even those coming from within Azure, are preconfigured in Azure SQL Database. When you create a new Azure SQL Database server in the Azure Preview Portal, the default setting is to grant access to the server to any Azure service included in your subscription, such as your Azure Website.

You must change the server firewall to permit access from the specified IP address (or range) in order to access the Azure SQL Database server from outside of Azure, such as using SQL Server Management Studio (SSMS). Choose the SQL server name in the Summary section of the Database blade.

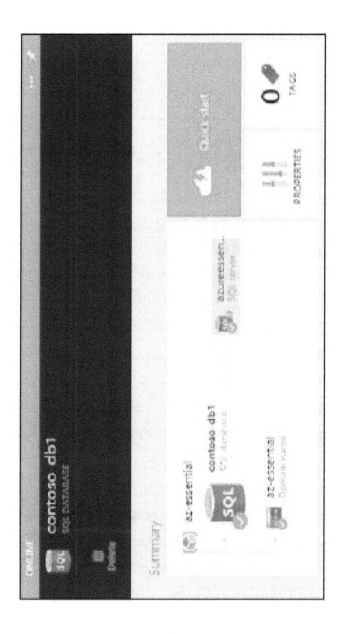

213

By doing this, you may access a new blade that lets you control the firewall settings and other features of the Azure SQL Database server. To open the Firewall Settings blade, select the Firewall Settings section.

You can create rules to permit access to the server from a certain IP address or enable or prevent Azure service access to the server on the Firewall Settings blade. You must set ALLOW ACCESS TO AZURE SERVICES to ON if you are hosting other Azure services (such as Azure Websites, Cloud Services, etc.) that require access to the Azure SQL Database instance.

TIP: It is now possible to set database-level firewall rules in addition to the server-level firewall rules accessible in the Azure Management Portal. T-SQL statements can be used to programmatically set database-level firewall rules.

HOW TO USE SQL SERVER MANAGEMENT STUDIO TO ESTABLISH A CONNECTION

Open SQL Server Management Studio after adding your IP address to the list of permitted IP addresses. You must be aware of the Azure SQL Database server's whole name. the Properties blade displays the complete server name in

214

addition to other crucial data. Clicking the PROPERTIES section of the Database blade will open the Properties blade.

Enter the complete server name, choose SQL Server Authentication, and enter the administrative login and password you selected when creating the database when the Connect To Server dialog box in SQL Server Management Studio appears.

INVOICING

Unlike on-premises SQL Server or SQL Server in an Azure virtual machine, Azure SQL Database is offered as a service, therefore there isn't a separate SQL Server license. Rather, the highest Azure SQL Database service tier utilized during the hour determines your hourly fee (keep in mind that you can switch tiers at any moment). For instance, you are billed the S3 rate for the full hour if you begin with an S1 at 3 p.m. then switch to an S3 at 3:20 p.m. After the tier or performance level modification is finished, the price adjustment takes effect.

It is crucial to comprehend the pricing of Azure SQL Database as well as the maximum number of databases that can be purchased. After all, the amount you spend will be directly impacted by the quantity of databases you have. Each subscription is limited to a maximum of six logical

215

Azure SQL Database servers by default. A maximum of 150 databases may be hosted on each server. By sending a support case to Azure Support, it is frequently possible to raise the default restrictions, which are soft limits.

CONTINUITY OF BUSINESS

Azure SQL Database offers a variety of choices to meet business continuity needs. Redundancy in the infrastructure is one method Azure SQL Database offers security. A hardware failure (hard drive, network, complete servers, etc.) could occur at any time in an Azure datacenter. By maintaining copies of the data on physically distinct nodes, Azure SQL Database offers high availability in the event of such hardware failures. One primary and two secondary replicas are the three database nodes, or replicas, that are always operational. Before a write operation is deemed complete, data must be written to both the primary and one of the secondary replicas. When something goes wrong, Azure SQL Database recognizes it and switches to the backup replica. If required, a fresh.

After that, a replica is made. Moreover, database recovery and disaster recovery are two common categories of business continuity in relation to databases. The capacity to reduce risk and recover from database corruption or an inadvertent

216

change or deletion of data is known as database recovery. Point in Time Restore is a function offered by Azure SQL Database to aid with database recovery. You can restore a database to any earlier point in time using Point in Time Restore. Depending on the Azure SQL Database tier you have chosen, you have a different amount of time to restore: 7 days for Basic, 15 days for Standard, and 35 days for Premium.

You can specify the name of the restored database (or leave it at the default name that is generated automatically) and the restoration point (date and time, at one-minute intervals) when you click the restoration button. This will open a new blade. The restoration process can take a while to finish. The size of the database, the restore point time chosen, and the activity log that must be replayed in order to reach the restore point are some of the variables that affect the precise time to restore, making it challenging to forecast. This procedure could take many hours for certain huge databases. From the portal's main Notifications blade, you may keep an eye on the completion status.

A database can be restored in its entirety if it has been erased. To accomplish this, choose the Operations section from the SQL Server blade after first choosing the Azure SQL

217

Database server that housed the database. This will launch a new Deleted Databases blade.

Choose the database that needs to be restored if more than one was erased. Give the database to be restored a name on the resultant Restore blade. Only the point at which the database was erased can be recovered. The restore request will be submitted once you click Create. The process of restoring a destroyed database may take a long time, much like a point-in-time restoration.

When a database needs to be restored to a known good point—which is frequently required due to user error—Point in Time Restore is useful. But catastrophe recovery is another facet of company continuity, and this is just one of them. The ability to return operations to a functional state in the event that a calamity makes the primary region unrecoverable is known as disaster recovery. When creating a disaster recovery plan, Azure SQL Database offers a number of tools that can be useful: Geo-Restore, Standard and Active Geo-Replication, and Database Copy and Export.

A COPY OF THE DATABASE

On the same Azure SQL Database server or on a different

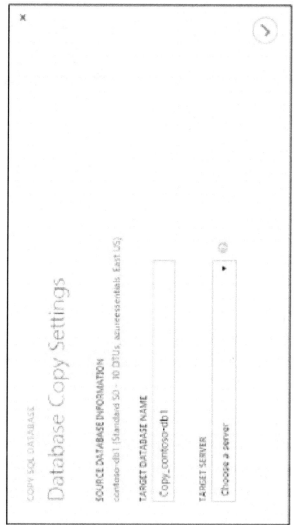

server in a different Azure region, Database Copy makes a

219

copy of the specified database. After the copy process is finished, the copy is transactionally consistent with the source. You will need to use the Azure Management Portal in order to perform a database copy. After selecting the desired database, click the COPY button on the bottom command bar to bring up the Database Copy Settings dialog box. Here, you may enter the Target Database Name and the Target Server. The DATABASES list in the portal allows you to track the Database Copy progress.

HOW TO IMPORT AND EXPORT

You can export an Azure SQL database into a BACPAC file using Import and Export. Azure Blob storage is where the BACPAC file is stored. A copy of the source from the moment the BACPAC was formed can then be created by importing the BACPAC file to a different server. Note that a transactionally consistent copy of the source database is not guaranteed by the export procedure. As a result, it is advised that you make a copy first, which does offer transactional consistency, and then export.

Take note: Remember that in Azure Blob storage, a BACPAC file is stored as a block blob. Block blobs can only be 200 GB in size. Therefore, you might not be able to export your database as a BACPAC file if it is larger than 200 GB.

220

Because the BACPAC file is a compressed copy of the database (data and schema), the precise maximum size varies.

You must use the Azure Management Portal in order to export an Azure SQL database. Choose the database you want to export after going to the SQL Databases section. Click EXPORT on the bottom command bar in the DASHBOARD section. Give the exported BACPAC file a name, choose an Azure Storage account that already exists or create a new one, and provide the administrative login and password for the Azure SQL Database server in the Export Database Settings dialog box that appears.

You can set up and schedule automatic exports in addition to on-demand exports. Choose the database of your choice in the Azure Management Portal, then navigate to the CONFIGURE area. Set the export status to AUTOMATIC instead of NONE. Enter the database credentials, export frequency, retention term, and name of the Azure Storage account to be used.

A new Azure SQL database can be created using the exported database. Click NEW in the lower-left corner of the Azure Management Portal, then select DATA SERVICES, SQL DATABASE, and IMPORT. you will need to choose

221

the target Azure subscription, server, and performance level, as well as go to the BACPAC file in Azure Blob storage and give the new database a name in the following Specify Database Settings dialog box.

Take note: Point in Time Restore is the suggested method for recovering from database corruption or unintentional data loss in Basic, Standard, and Premium databases. Note that Web and Business edition databases do not support Point in Time Restore. Database Copy and Export will still be your best option if you need to maintain a backup copy of the database for a longer amount of time than the Point in Time Restore retention term (7 days for Basic, 15 days for Standard, and 35 days for Premium).

CONVENTIONAL GEO-REPLICATION

One offline secondary database can be created in the parent database's associated datacenter using standard geo-replication. Until the area housing the original database fails, clients cannot connect to the secondary database. The cost of the secondary database is 75 percent of that of the primary database.

GEO-REPLICATION IN ACTION

You can establish up to four readable secondary databases across several Azure regions using Active Geo-Replication, a functionality that is exclusive to Premium tier databases. Unlike Standard Geo-Replication, you are in charge of deciding when to fail over one of the secondary databases. The main is charged at the same rate as each legible secondary.

Choose the desired database using the Azure Preview Portal to enable Standard or Active Geo-Replication. You can see a map showing any secondary databases that are currently in place or, if none are, an option to configure geo-replication from the Geo Replication section. To launch a new Geo Replication blade, select the Geo Replication section (which shows the map). You can choose the preferred spot after viewing all of the possible secondary locations on this blade. Keep in mind that only the paired area will be accessible for a Standard database. But from a Premium database, you may choose from any of the places that are offered. Either choose from the list of TARGET REGIONS shown on the blade, or click the area on the map. By doing this, a new Create Secondary blade will open, enabling you to set up secondary database attributes.

The SECONDARY TYPE will only be set to Non-Readable by default for Standard Geo-Replication. You can choose from a variety of Azure regions for the REGION when using

223

Active Geo-Replication, and the SECONDARY TYPE will be set to Readable by default.

THE GEO-RESTORE

Lastly, you can restore an Azure SQL database from a backup to any Azure SQL Database server in any Azure region using the Geo-Restore functionality in Azure SQL Database. The database size, performance level, and quantity of concurrent restore requests in the target Azure region will all affect the restoration time. Azure SQL Database automatically creates backups of all databases, enabling both Point in Time Restore (as covered earlier in this chapter) and Geo-Restore. Every five minutes, transaction log backups are made, differential backups are made once a day, and full backups are made once a week. The backup data is stored in a geo-redundant paired area (such as North Europe and West Europe, East US and West US, etc.) in Azure Blob storage (RA-GRS).

224

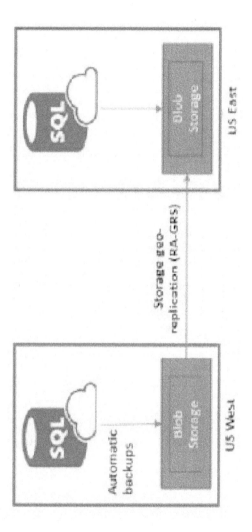

To begin, choose the Azure SQL Database server you want to restore by navigating to it. Choose BACKUPS from the top menu on the server screen, and then click RESTORE in the command bar at the bottom.

Enter the new database name and choose the target server (either choose an existing one or build a new one) in the resultant Specify Restore Settings dialog box. To send the restore request, click the checkmark. When choosing which feature or features to include in your disaster recovery plan, the recovery time goal (RTO) and recovery point objective (RPO) are crucial considerations. After a disaster, the RTO shows the maximum amount of downtime before the application is operational. Before the application is operational following a disaster, the RPO specifies the maximum amount of recent data loss (in terms of time).

SERVICE LEVEL CONTRACT

For Basic, Standard, and Premium tiers, Microsoft offers a database connectivity SLA of 99.99 percent. The SLA does not apply to any performance goals for the different tiers; rather, it solely applies to the ability to connect to the database.

APPLICATIONS THAT LINK TO THE AZURE SQL DATABASE

Popular programming languages like PHP, Java,.NET, and many more can be used for creating applications that must connect to an Azure SQL database. Additionally supported is Entity Framework, beginning with.NET Framework 3.5 Service Pack 1. The connection string is among the first items you'll need. As previously shown, you can see the connection string from the Azure Preview Portal by selecting the PROPERTIES section of the selected database blade. A new Database Connection Strings blade will open when you click the Show Database Connection Strings link under CONNECTION STRINGS. This blade will display the connection string in several forms, such as ADO.NET, PHP, JDBC, and ODBC (which is compatible with node.js applications).

The Azure SQL Database connection string is comparable to the SQL Server connection string. The connection string format for ADO.NET, for instance, is as follows:

```
"Server=tcp:{your_servername_here}.database.windows.net,1433;Database={your_database_name_here};
User ID={your_username_here}@{your_servername_here};
Password={your_password_here};Trusted_Connection=False;Encrypt=True;Connection Timeout=30;".
```

Keep in mind that the connection string sets the Encrypt property to True and the Trusted_Connection property to False. This is to offer extra security when using the Internet

228

to access Azure SQL Database. By doing this, possible man-in-the-middle attacks are thwarted. Regardless of the option, Azure SQL Database will actually require an encrypted connection.

Protecting your code from temporary failures is crucial when writing code against an Azure SQL database. Intermittent errors are known as transient errors, and they usually go away if the command is tried again. Compared to databases, Azure SQL Database has a higher frequency of these issues with the use of a local area network. This is because the Internet is an inherently unreliable network, and because Azure SQL Database is a managed service, it may occasionally experience maintenance issues that result in momentary connection outages. When establishing connections or running commands against an Azure SQL database, applications should use retry logic to anticipate and protect against temporary problems. Entity Framework 6 has connection resiliency/retry logic for .NET apps that use it. This logic will identify temporary problems from the Azure SQL Database and try the command again. The Transient Fault Handling Application Block is an application block found in Microsoft Patterns & Practices' Enterprise Libraries 5 and 6.

Retry commands and the detection of temporary errors are further uses for this module.

230

CHAPTER EIGHT

AZURE VIRTUAL MACHINES' SQL SERVER

Even though Azure SQL Database offers database-as-a-service with enterprise-grade functionality and almost no administration, there are still circumstances where you need to run your own SQL Server configuration. Hosting your own SQL Server implementation has many benefits. The need to utilize functionalities that Azure SQL Database does not offer is a frequent justification.

You may host and manage your own virtual machines (VMs) with Azure Virtual Machines, as covered in Chapter 3. Installing, configuring, and managing your own entire SQL Server virtual machine (VM) or cluster of VMs is primarily your job.

INVOICING

There are three crucial cost considerations to make when executing your own SQL Server install on Azure Virtual Machines. The price of the Windows virtual machine itself comes first. Keep in mind that Azure virtual machines are billed on a usage-per-minute basis. The cost of a SQL Server license comes in second. You will be charged a per-minute SQL Server license fee when utilizing a SQL Server image from the Azure Virtual Machines image gallery. This fee varies based on the target VM size and the SQL Server version (Web, Standard, or Enterprise). Lastly, you will also be responsible for paying for Azure Storage. The persistence mechanism for Azure Virtual Machines disks is Azure Storage, more especially page blobs. on summary, Total Cost = Windows Server cost + SQL Server licensing cost + Azure Storage cost is how the price of SQL Server on Azure Virtual Machines may be expressed.

Instead of paying the per-minute fee for utilizing a SQL Server license that you got from an Azure Virtual Machines image, you can use your own SQL Server license. Only the Windows Server license and any associated Azure Storage fees are paid in this scenario. One benefit of License Mobility via Microsoft's Software Assurance on Azure service is the opportunity to use your own SQL Server license.

CONFIGURING A VIRTUAL MACHINE

There are a few crucial factors to consider when setting up SQL Server on Azure Virtual Machines.

- **VM-related factors**: For SQL Server Standard Edition, use a virtual machine (VM) of A2 or higher. To reduce latency, keep the virtual machine and storage account in the same Azure region.

232

Additionally, because consistent write order across disks is not guaranteed, disable geo-replication if database data and log files are being stored on several data drives.

- **Disk-related factors**: To store database data and log files, use a data disk with the cache policy set to None. Log files and database data shouldn't be kept on the D drive. The D drive is not persistent to Azure Blob storage; it is a physical temporary disk. On the other hand, you might think about keeping the tempdb database on the D drive if you're running a D-series virtual machine. Because the D disk in D-series virtual machines is an SSD, tempdb performance may be enhanced. You can attach additional data disks (up to the maximum permitted by the VM size) and utilize disk striping to improve IOPS for workloads that above the 500 IOPS limit for a single data disk. Also See For a thorough analysis of SQL Server performance best practices in Azure Virtual Machines.

CONTINUITY OF BUSINESS

When you run SQL Server in Azure Virtual Machines, you can use the majority of the high availability and disaster

233

recovery (HADR) solutions you might use for on-premises SQL Server deployments. However, why is HADR for SQL Server in Azure Virtual Machines a concern? Azure offers high-availability options for virtual machines (VMs), as covered in Chapter 3, but not always for SQL Server that runs in the VM. The SQL Server instance may be unavailable, unwell, or both, even when the virtual machine is online. Additionally, software updates or hardware malfunctions could make the virtual machine unavailable. Therefore, a well-practiced HADR approach ought to be taken into account.

Many of the HADR features that are available for on-premises SQL Server deployments are also supported by SQL Server in Azure Virtual Machines, including AlwaysOn, database mirroring, log shipping, and backup and restore to Azure Blob storage.

Establishing a hybrid topology to enable the HADR technology to span between an Azure region and an on-premises datacenter may be feasible, depending on the technology being utilized. A topology that spans several Azure regions is possible with certain configurations, including SQL Server AlwaysOn.

234

COMPARING SQL SERVER ON AZURE VIRTUAL MACHINES WITH AZURE SQL DATABASE

It can be challenging to decide whether to utilize SQL Server in Azure Virtual Machines or Azure SQL Database. On the one hand, because Azure SQL Database handles numerous operations like updates, patching, backups, and business continuity scenarios automatically, it is perfect for lowering the administrative costs associated with provisioning and administering relational databases. However, SQL Server on Azure Virtual Machines offers the ability to move or expand current SQL Server workloads from on-premises to Azure. For certain individuals and situations, the opportunity to have fine-grained control over those operations may outweigh the higher administrative costs associated with operating SQL Server in Azure Virtual Machines. While there are many similarities between Azure SQL Database and SQL Server, there are also some significant differences, particularly with regard to SQL Server functionality that Azure SQL Database does not yet support.

These include the following:

- Windows authentication.
- Dispersed transactions.
- Data from Filestream.

- Search in full text.

- Types Defined by the User (UDTs).

- Encryption of Transparent Data (TDE).

- Mirroring of databases.

- Prolonged stored processes.

There is no support for SQL Server Integration Services (SSIS) or SQL Server Reporting Services (SSRS). As an alternative, connect to an Azure SQL database while running SQL Server on-premises or in an Azure virtual machine. USE statements are not supported by T-SQL features. A fresh connection needs to be made in order to switch databases.

CLR stands for Common Language Runtime queries that are distributed (multipart). Additionally, Azure SQL Database has various general restrictions and specifications that set it apart from a conventional SQL Server. These include the following:

- Clustered indexes are required for all Azure SQL Database tables. Until a clustered index is constructed, insert operations will not be permitted.

- When a connection is inactive for longer than half an hour, it is automatically closed.

- Only connections on port 1433, which is a standard port for SQL Server, are accepted by Azure SQL

236

Database. Make sure that outgoing TCP connections on port 1433 are permitted by your firewall.

- Some tools may need to add the server name to the login because of variations in how the TDS protocol is implemented: [login]@[name of server]

Choosing between Azure SQL Database and SQL Server in Azure Virtual Machines involves a number of considerations, including **database size, whether the application is new or existing, the degree of administrative control (including hardware infrastructure), business continuity plan, and hybrid scenarios**, to mention a few. For cloud-designed apps that don't use unsupported capabilities and where near-zero management is a top concern, Azure SQL Database is frequently the best option. For new or existing applications that need a high degree of control and customization (i.e., full compatibility with SQL Server) and for which it is desired to no longer maintain on-premises hardware, SQL Server on Azure Virtual Machines is frequently the best option.

ALTERNATIVES TO DATABASES

- **MySQL**: MySQL is another well-known relational database. The ClearDb database-as-a-service for

MySQL from SuccessBricks is now available on the Azure platform thanks to a partnership between Microsoft and the company. Click the green NEW button on the Azure Preview Portal to begin. In the list of services that are offered, locate the MySQL Database feature.

238

You will be able to enter crucial information about your new MySQL database, such as the following, when the New MySQL Database blade opens:

- **Name of the Database:** What's the new database called?
- **Pricing Tier:** Pick a pricing tier from the list of options. These tiers have nothing to do with the performance levels or tiers of the Azure SQL Database.
- **Resource Group:** The Azure SQL Database will be housed in either an existing or newly created logical group. Grouping relevant Azure resources together is made easier with resource groups.
- **Membership:** The Azure subscription that was desired.
- **Legal Phrases:** To proceed, you must accept the legal terms, which specify that SuccessBricks, not Microsoft, is the provider of the service.

When you're done, submit the request to build the new MySQL database by clicking the blue build button at the bottom of the blade. The database blade will open automatically after the database has been built. You can inspect information about the new MySQL Database, including the entire hostname, username, password, connection string, and more, by clicking the Properties section, which will open a new blade.

OPTIONS FOR NOSQL

For your database requirements, you are not need to use Azure SQL Database or SQL Server in Azure Virtual Machines. DocumentDB and Azure Table storage are the two NoSQL solutions offered by Azure.

DOCUMENTDB

The Azure platform offers DocumentDB, a NoSQL document database service that is completely managed and extremely scalable. All JSON documents contributed to the database are automatically indexed by DocumentDB, which was built to accommodate JSON documents natively. To query the documents, you utilize well-known SQL syntax. As this article is being done, DocumentDB is under Preview.

STORAGE FOR TABLES

Azure One of the most affordable and scalable key/value NoSQL stores on the Azure platform is table storage. A single subscription supports 100 storage accounts, and table storage can store up to 500 TB per storage account. A partition key and a row key serve as the main composite

240

index for the table in table storage, a semistructured NoSQL data store.

ACTIVE DIRECTORY ON AZURE

Who we are and what we do are defined by our identity. The core of many services and applications is identity. Identity provides information about who used the program and what the user is capable of doing. Applications frequently lose the intimacy or personal connection that so many users find appealing when they lack identification. program managers find it more challenging to identify who utilized their program and what the users were able to accomplish when they lack identity.

Azure Active Directory (Azure AD) is at the heart of the Microsoft Azure platform's identity story. Azure AD offers a contemporary identity solution that is safe, scalable, and compatible with both on-premises and cloud-hosted systems.

AN OVERVIEW OF AZURE ACTIVE DIRECTORY

It can be useful to know what Azure AD is not before talking about what it is. First off, Windows Server Active Directory cannot be replaced by Azure AD. You cannot domain join physical or virtual computers to Azure AD as it stands right now. Printers and other items cannot be assigned to Azure

241

AD. If you require Windows Server Active Directory's whole functionality, you might want to install and set it up on Azure Virtual Machines.

AZURE ACTIVE DIRECTORY: WHAT IS IT?

Azure AD is a multitenant directory service that offers cloud-based identity and access management that is reliable and secure. Actually, a lot of Microsoft's high-end cloud services, like Office 365, Dynamics CRM Online, Windows Intune, and of course, Azure, are stored in Azure AD. Azure AD is an Azure service that offers identity and access management for on-premises systems, much like Windows Server Active Directory does. However, Microsoft is in charge of overseeing the complete Azure AD infrastructure (high availability, scalability, disaster recovery, etc.) rather than you taking on the task of installing and configuring the numerous servers required for on-premises Active Directory. You, as a user of the Azure AD service (directory-as-a-service), determine which users and the data associated with them should be in the directory, as well as who can access the data and what apps can access it.

It is not appropriate to think about Azure AD as a substitute for Windows Server Active Directory. Rather, Azure AD is an add-on service. Using a solution like Azure Active

242

Directory Sync (AADSync), users and groups can be synchronized to your Azure AD directory if you already have Active Directory on-premises. The DirSync tool was the forerunner to AADSync.

To enable single sign-on (SSO), Azure AD can be linked to an on-premises Active Directory. This can be either shared sign-on, where a password hash is synchronized between Active Directory and Azure AD using AADSync, or true SSO, which federates the on-premises identity to Azure AD using Active Directory Federation Services (AD FS). Because AADSync replicates password changes by default every three hours, shared sign-on is easier to set up at the expense of a slight lag in password change synchronization.

A multitenant directory service is Azure AD. When you sign up for a Microsoft cloud service (Office 365, Azure, etc.), you acquire a dedicated instance of Azure AD for each tenant. Each tenant directory is separate from the others in the service and made to prevent other tenants from accessing user data. This means that unless an administrator gives specific permission, others cannot access data in your directory.

Remember that Azure AD isn't limited to cloud or Azure-hosted solutions. Both on-premises and cloud solutions

243

(hosted in Azure or elsewhere) can use Azure AD. Azure AD is accessible through a contemporary REST API, as opposed to on-premises Active Directory, which is accessed through technologies like Kerberos or Lightweight Directory Access Protocol (LDAP). This makes it possible for a variety of applications, including cloud, mobile, and on-premises ones, to access the rich data found in the Azure AD directory. This gives developers access to a wide range of opportunities that were previously unattainable or challenging to do with on-premises solutions. Developers can quickly set up SSO for cloud apps and query and write (create, update, delete) against the directory data by utilizing Azure AD and its Graph REST API.

EDITIONS OF ACTIVE DIRECTORY

There are three Azure AD tiers as of this writing:

- Free offers features like user management, synchronization with on-premises Active Directory, Office 365 and Azure SSO, and access to SaaS apps in the Azure AD application gallery.
- In addition to self-service password resets, group-based application access, configurable branding, and a 99.9 percent availability SLA, Basic offers all the benefits of the Free tier.

244

- In addition to self-service group management, multi-factor authentication, advanced security reports and alerts, Microsoft Forefront Identity Manager (Microsoft Identity Manager) licenses, and future enterprise features like password write-back, Premium offers all the features of the Free and Basic tiers.

MAKING A DIRECTORY

Making your own Azure AD directory is simple. As was previously indicated, you already have an Azure AD directory if you are utilizing a Microsoft cloud service, such Office 365. An existing directory that is used to authenticate with other Microsoft cloud services can be linked to a new Azure subscription. To accomplish this, use your current work or school account—formerly known as an organizational account—to log into the Azure Management Portal).

The portal will provide a notice stating that there are no subscriptions linked to your account if there aren't any Azure subscriptions currently associated with it. You must first create an Azure subscription. After you've set up for an Azure subscription, you can access it using your work or school account.

245

No subscriptions found.

SIGN OUT ⊕

SIGN UP FOR WINDOWS AZURE ⊕

WINDOWS AZURE HOME PAGE ⊕

CONTACT SUPPORT ⊕

Before you can start using Windows Azure, you need to get a subscription.

We were unable to find any Azure subscriptions where you are a service administrator or co-administrator.

You are signed as karen@azure-essentials.com in the directory azureessentials.onmicrosoft.com (Azure Essentials). If this was not the account you intended to use, please sign out and sign in again using the intended account.

246

An Azure AD directory will be created automatically when you join up for a Microsoft cloud service, such as Office 365 or Azure, if you do not already have a subscription. Azure needs a directory in order to function. The Azure Management Portal allows you to link your subscription to a different Azure AD directory. Click EDIT DIRECTORY on the bottom command bar after choosing your subscription under the SETTINGS extension in the left navigation box. The outcome

You can choose a different Azure AD directory to be linked to the chosen Azure subscription using the dialog box. The Azure Management Portal allows you to add a new Azure AD directory. To accomplish this, click the +NEW button in the bottom command bar, then pick APP SERVICE, ACTIVE DIRECTORY, DIRECTORY, and lastly CUSTOM CREATE. Choose your country or region, give the directory a nice name, and enter a unique domain name in the subsequent Add Directory dialog box.

PERSONALIZED DOMAINS
Take note of the directory's domain name, [directory_name](dot)onmicrosoft(dot)com.

The *.onmicrosoft.com domain is linked to a unique name for each Azure AD directory.

The *.onmicrosoft.com domain name is not required to be used at all times. Alternatively, a custom domain that you own can be assigned. Users in the directory would instead use the custom domain name once it was created. It's not too difficult to link a custom domain to your Azure AD directory. An intuitive wizard will guide you through each step in the Azure AD area of the Azure Management Portal. Three fundamental steps are involved:

- Learn the fundamentals of your domain (or, if necessary, get a new one).
- Establish a DNS record to demonstrate domain ownership.
- Confirm the domain name.
- Click DOMAINS in the top navigation section after first choosing the relevant directory in the Azure AD part of the Azure Management Portal.
- If you don't already have a custom domain, the portal will ask you to establish one and offer you with a link to ADD A CUSTOM DOMAIN to get you started.

A dialog box will appear when you click the ADD A CUSTOM DOMAIN link, asking you to add the preferred

248

domain name to the list of possible domain names connected to your Azure AD directory. Demonstrating your ownership of the domain name will be the next step. Adding a DNS configuration (TXT or MX record) at your domain name registrar is the second step of the procedure. Although GoDaddy is utilized in this example, the wizard offers a link to an MSDN article that offers comprehensive instructions for a number of well-known registrars.

To interact with DNS records for GoDaddy, navigate to the DNS Manager area. If that was the record type you chose in the Azure Management Portal, you will need to add a new TXT record there. Enter the Host, TXT Value, and TTL parameters that were also entered in the Azure Management Portal wizard.

Make sure to save the zone file after clicking Finish in the GoDaddy editor. Once the zone file has been saved and the TXT record has been added, you may click VERIFY in the Azure Management Portal wizard to try to validate the domain. You will be notified if the verification is successful. The DNS updates may not take effect for 15 minutes. In certain situations, the DNS records may not propagate for up to 72 hours. You should go back to the domain registrar website to confirm the DNS record information is accurate if, after 72 hours, you are still unable to verify the domain. Once you exit the wizard, the DOMAINS section should display both the custom domain and the default (or basic) domain. Click the ADD button in the bottom command bar to begin the process of adding more custom domains. You can modify the principal domain linked to the default *.onmicrosoft.com domain by adding additional custom, verified domains.

REMOVE A DIRECTORY

A maximum of 20 directories can be created (or associated with, including being a member of). In development and testing environments when you might not have access to the production subscription, it can be useful to create additional Azure AD folders. You can quickly remove a directory once you're done with it. A few requirements (imposed by Azure) must be fulfilled in order to delete a directory because it is a potentially important action:

- The global administrator is the only user in the directory.
- The directory contains no applications.

There are no subscriptions linked to the directory, such as Office 365, Azure, etc. The directory does not have any Multi-Factor Authentication providers connected. Simply

250

choose the directory and click DELETE in the command bar
at the bottom to remove it.

CHAPTER NINE

GROUPS AND USERS

Adding users to the Azure AD directory is a typical next step after building the directory. Users can utilize Azure AD capabilities like SSO, application gallery access, and Multi-Factor Authentication once they are in the directory; further information on these features is given later in this chapter.

INCLUDE USERS

There are three categories of users in Azure AD: A user within your company Your directory is where the user is created and maintained. A user who has an account with Microsoft (hotmail.com, outlook.com, etc.) By giving the user co-administrative privileges to the Azure subscription, this is frequently done as a means of facilitating collaboration on Azure resources. An individual in a different Azure AD directory Another Azure AD directory is the source of the user. There are several methods you can use to add new users to the directory:

- The directory may have users because it was created using a Microsoft cloud service, such Office 365.
- AADSync allows users to be synchronized from an on-premises instance of Windows Server Active Directory.

252

- Programmatic user addition is possible with PowerShell or the Azure AD Graph REST API. Through the Azure Management Portal, users can be manually added.

Your user account will be the only one in the directory when you first create a new Azure AD directory and utilize an Azure subscription linked to a Microsoft account. Next, you may add users to the directory by selecting the ADD USER button on the bottom command bar once you've navigated to the USERS section of the selected directory. You can enter information for the new user in a new dialog box that appears when you click the ADD USER button. You can choose the domain name suffix for a user who works for your company, such as *.onmicrosoft.com by default or a custom domain (if set).

The next stage allows you to provide further details about the user, including their display name, first and last names, and possibly an administrative job. Additionally, you can allow the user to use Multi-Factor Authentication.

Obtaining a temporary password for the user is the last step in creating a new user in your company. A temporary password is produced and assigned to the newly created user when the CREATE button is clicked.

The password appears once the temporary password has been created and assigned, and you may choose to have it forwarded to you via email. Show the temporary password and send it if you like. Adding a new user who already has a Microsoft account follows a similar procedure. You will use

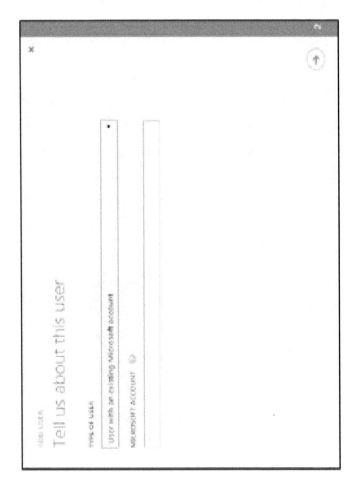

254

the user's Microsoft account (email address) in place of assigning them to a domain name linked to your company. Similar to adding a user to your organization, you can provide the user's first and last names, display name, and role after giving their email address. Lastly, you must supply the user's name when adding a new (external) user who already has an account in another Azure AD directory. As shown in This is accomplished using the user's email account (or, in Active Directory terminology, the user's User Principal Name, or UPN). Remember that you must also be an administrator in the other Azure AD directory in order to choose a user there. The display name and user name from the source or home directory are copied to your directory when you add an external user. Any modifications to the user's properties (email address, display name, job title, etc.) do not spread to your directory, but the user would still authenticate against his or her home directory.

Examine the SOURCED FROM column in the USERS section to find out where users in the directory came from. The SOURCED FROM field would show Local Active Directory if users were synchronized from a Windows Server Active Directory using AADSync. Likewise, the value Office 365 in the SOURCED FROM column would belong to customers of Office 365.

255

INCLUDE GROUPS

Putting users into groups is a standard procedure in Active Directory. Assigning permissions or granting access to resources is made simpler by groups. Access is given to the group that the user is a member of rather than to each individual user. The group's access privileges are passed down to the user. In an Azure AD directory, groups may also be created and managed. When granting access to Software-as-a-Service (SaaS) apps found in the Azure AD application gallery (covered later in this chapter), groups in Azure AD can be useful. You can create and manage groups in the GROUPS section of the chosen Azure AD directory. Select the ADD GROUP button on the bottom command bar or select the ADD A GROUP link to establish a group if none already exists.

You can give the new group a name and description in the Add Group dialog box. To add users to the group, click the ADD MEMBERS button on the bottom command bar or the ADD MEMBERS link after selecting the group name to bring up a new page where you may administer the group. You can choose users or other groups in the current directory to add as members to the group you've chosen using the Add Members dialog box

256

AUTHENTICATION USING MULTIPLE FACTORS

Additional security for on-premises or Azure-hosted products is offered via Azure Multi-Factor Authentication (MFA). The only solutions covered in this chapter are those hosted on Azure. In order for Azure MFA to function, a second authentication challenge must be successfully injected by the user. Azure MFA adds a challenge based on something you have, such a phone call, text message, or mobile app notification, to the password-based authentication challenge (something you know). It is more difficult for hackers to infiltrate and gain access to the account when there are several layers of protection in place. There are several variants of MFA. While Azure AD Premium provides MFA support for users, Azure AD Free and Azure AD Basic support MFA for Azure administrators. MFA for Azure administrators adds security to the creation and management of resources like Azure Websites and Azure Virtual Machines by protecting their administrative account. When users sign into apps that enable Azure AD, MFA for users adds an extra layer of security.

MULTI-FACTOR AUTHENTICATION ON AZURE

257

Jason Taylor

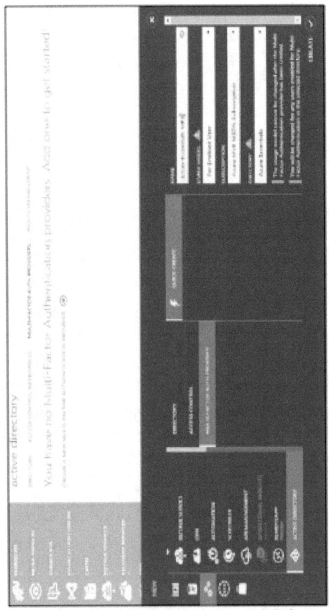

You must first add an MFA Provider in Azure AD before you
258

can start utilizing Azure MFA's full potential. Go to the Azure Management Portal's ACTIVE DIRECTORY section and select the MULTI-FACTOR AUTH PROVIDER section to add an MFA Provider. If there aren't any providers, you can choose to make one.

Clicking the MANAGE option opens a new browser window that launches the Azure Multi-Factor Authentication administration interface, allowing you to adjust many of the service's advanced capabilities after creating a new MFA provider.

Azure administrators can use multi-factor authentication. As you may remember from previously in this chapter, you could choose to enable MFA when you created a new user. Choosing the user's name and then clicking the MANAGE MULTI-FACTOR AUTH button on the command bar opens a new browser window with a website that lets you control MFA settings. As an alternative, you can utilize this website to enable MFA if the user isn't already, by choosing the user or users you want and clicking Enable.

An extra security verification step will be shown to the user if MFA is enabled and they try to access the Azure management portal (the user must also be a co-administrator on the Azure subscription). The user will be prompted to select the preferred contact mode (phone, text message, or

mobile application) and follow the instructions when they attempt to log in for the first time. The user will be required to supply the desired additional security verification answer on subsequent login attempts. A text message verification code is requested.

GALLERY OF APPLICATIONS

More than 2,400 (and counting) well-known SaaS apps, including Box, DocuSign, Salesforce, Google Apps, and many more, are available through the Azure AD application gallery. Azure AD streamlines the process by providing SSO for the apps, saving IT managers from having to configure access to each one independently and maybe managing many different logins.

Three SSO options are supported by Azure AD:

- Azure AD Single Sign-On makes use of the user's Azure AD account details. The user does not have to reauthenticate in order to access the third-party SaaS application if they are already logged into Azure AD (or Office 365). Federation-based SSO is supported by a small number of apps in the Azure AD application gallery.
- The password Single Sign-On makes use of the user's third-party SaaS application account details. This

method uses a web browser extension to gather, safely store, and send the user's account details and password to the SaaS application. This type of SSO is supported by most apps in the Azure AD application gallery. Chrome (Windows 7 or later; MacOS X or later) and Internet Explorer (IE8, IE9, and IE10 on Windows 7 or later) both support the browser extension.

- Current Active Directory Federation Services (AD FS) or another third-party provider is used for SSO in single sign-on.

HOW TO INCLUDE PROPOSALS FOR GALLERIES

Choose the relevant directory and then the APPLICATIONS section from the top navigation options to add gallery applications to your Azure AD directory. You have no apps in the gallery, click ADD AN APPLICATION to bring up a new dialog box with two choices: add an application from the gallery or add an application you are creating.

Choose the first option if you or another person in your company has created an application that wants to utilize Azure AD features (such as SSO, the ability to query the Azure AD Graph API, and so on). You can register third-party SaaS apps with your Azure AD

263

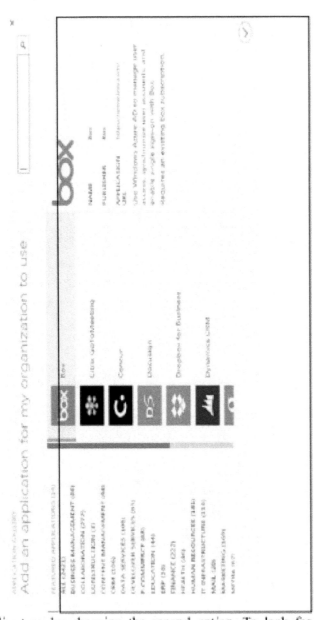

directory by choosing the second option. To look for a

264

particular application by name, use the filter box located in the top-right corner. Each application will show up on the list in the APPLICATIONS section once you have chosen the desired application or applications. To add an application, click ADD, and to remove an application, select it and click DELETE.

ASSIGNING USERS TO APPLICATIONS

Applications can use Azure AD for SSO in a variety of ways, as was previously discussed. For instance, Twitter only offers Password Single Sign-On and Existing Single Sign-On, but Box offers all three options (Azure AD Single Sign-On, Password Single Sign-On, and Existing Single Sign-On). Configure SSO for the chosen application by following the on-screen instructions.

Upon granting access to Azure AD, certain applications, like Box, can automatically provision (create) users into the application. Any changes made to a user's access or deletion from Azure AD are automatically reflected in the SaaS application. This can make the duties of IT administration easier. Click Assign Users first to bring up a new screen where you can assign or revoke access to the chosen application for Azure AD directory users. After choosing the

Jason Taylor

required user, click ASSIGN or REMOVE on the bottom

266

command bar.

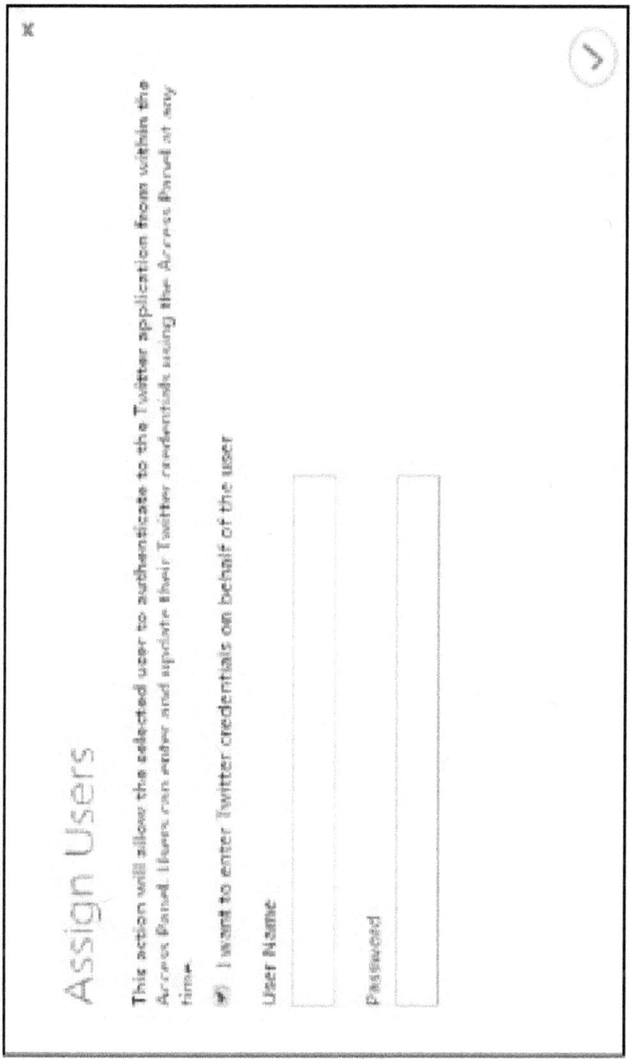

Assign Users

This action will allow the selected user to authenticate to the Twitter application from within the Access Panel. Users can enter and update their Twitter credentials using the Access Panel at any time.

◉ I want to enter Twitter credentials on behalf of the user

User Name

Password

Applications that use Password Single Sign-On will give you the choice to either let users enter and update their own credentials or enter them for them after you've assigned them.

MYAPPS

Users can access the SaaS apps from the MyApps for Azure Active Directory website at http://myapps(microsoft.com after being granted access to them through the Azure AD application gallery. To use the website, users must first login using their Azure AD credentials (either *.onmicrosoft.com or a related custom domain name). The user will be instantly logged into the MyApps site if they are already logged into one of the Microsoft cloud service sites (Office 365, Azure, etc.). The site is divided into two primary areas, Applications and Profile.

Each application to which the user has been allowed access is represented as a tile in the Applications section. The user may be asked to install a browser component the first time they visit the application if password-based SSO was chosen as the authentication mechanism when the application was added to the company's Azure AD directory.

The user only needs to click the tile of the selected program to access it. If password-based SSO was used, the user will

268

be asked to provide their SaaS application credentials (unless the administrator added the application on their behalf). After that, the user is taken to the application and given the necessary login information. A password changing option and other basic information about the current user are available in the Profile area.

TOOLS FOR MANAGEMENT

You have studied a number of the Microsoft Azure platform's key features in previous chapters of this book. Among many other things, you now know how to establish Azure SQL databases, storage accounts, virtual machines, cloud services, and websites. Most of the examples have shown how to use either the Azure Preview Portal or the Azure Management Portal. Other tools will be helpful throughout the construction and management of Azure resources, even though the portal or portals are an excellent method to deal with them.

OVERVIEW OF MANAGEMENT TOOLS

There are a ton of great tools available to help with Azure solution development or management; in fact, there are too many to discuss in this chapter. This chapter covers the Azure Cross-Platform Command-Line Interface (xplat-cli) tools, PowerShell, and Microsoft Visual Studio.

Visual Studio offers developers a comprehensive, integrated experience for creating, deploying, and maintaining Azure apps. The Azure PowerShell cmdlets and xplat-cli offer operations and IT professionals a stable and strong scripting environment for managing Azure resources. Actually, PowerShell is the only way to access some complex functionalities. Regardless of your operating system, the xplat-cli tools offer a straightforward yet effective way to manage Azure resources because they function similarly on Windows, Linux, and Mac computers.

The main tool used by Azure developers to create and manage Azure resources is probably Visual Studio. This is particularly true for developers working on projects utilizing the Microsoft technology stack (Windows,.NET, etc.). The xplat-cli will be the main focus of developers working with Mac or Linux platforms. Both Azure administration sites are accessible to developers and IT professionals.

HOW TO SET UP THE AZURE SDK

Installing the Microsoft Azure SDK for.NET is one of the first things an Azure developer should do after setting up Visual Studio. The Azure SDK is available for download from the Azure Downloads page at http://azure(dot)microsoft.com/en-us/downloads/.

270

Install the Visual Studio SDK that corresponds to your version of the program. Since this page is the source for several language SDKs (such as Java, PHP, Ruby, and others) as well as the PowerShell and Azure command-line interface tools, you should probably bookmark it because you will return to it frequently.

Any client libraries needed to work with Azure services, including Storage, Service Bus, Cloud Services, and others, are included in the SDK. Installing the SDK will also set up Visual Studio to fully support Azure Websites and Cloud Services for development and debugging. The SDK also comes with emulators for Storage and Compute, which are excellent for working on projects when you are unable to connect to the Internet (and hence Azure). Additionally, Web PI will install any required components. It will take a few minutes to complete the entire process. When you're done, a dialog box should appear, displaying the different items that are installed as part of the Microsoft Azure SDK for .NET.

HOW TO USE SERVER EXPLORER TO MANAGE RESOURCES

Once the Azure SDK is installed, navigate to Server Explorer. Azure will be a new node in Server Explorer. You may control different Azure resources from the Azure node in Server Explorer.

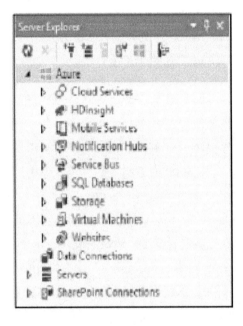

Connecting to your Azure subscription or subscriptions is the first step. To do this, right-click the Azure node and choose Connect To Microsoft Azure Subscription. This brings up a dialog box that asks for the email address associated with the account used to enter into Azure. The email address used to log into any of the Azure administration portals should be the same.

272

The required setup information to connect to any Azure accounts for whom the supplied email address is an administrator or co-administrator will be immediately downloaded by Visual Studio following authentication.

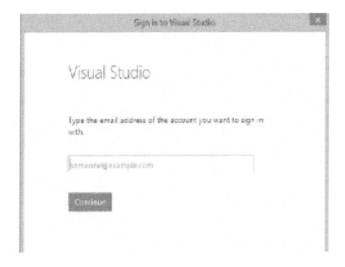

Subscriptions dialog box that appears when you right-click the Azure node and choose Manage Subscriptions. All of the subscriptions and Azure regions that you have access to through Visual Studio are displayed in this dialog box. Simply check the relevant boxes if you wish to exclude specific subscriptions or geographical areas from view while using Azure resources in Visual Studio.

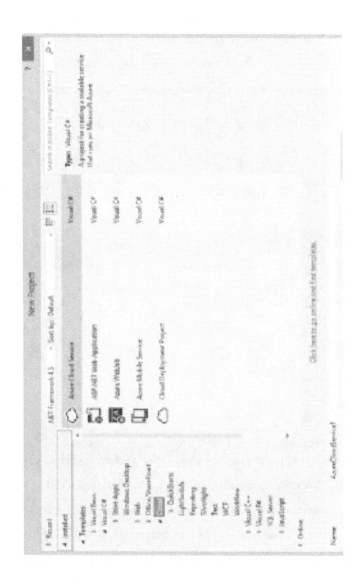

Simply expand the resource's node to manage it in Azure. Selecting and extending a node will provide additional

274

information about the resource, depending on the resource. Expanding Virtual Machines, for instance, displays the public endpoints; expanding Websites, on the other hand, displays details about the files and any associated WebJobs. Additionally, you can obtain extra contextual information by right-clicking on a node.

For instance, right-clicking a particular Websites node, will offer contextual information to access the site in a browser, connect a debugger, view streaming logs, and more. Additionally, you can use Server Explorer to create a new resource. To accomplish this, right-click on the resource of your choice and choose "Create a new resource." To establish a new Azure website, for instance, right-click the Websites node and choose establish New Site to launch the process.

HOW TO MAKE A RESOURCE IN AZURE

Visual Studio and the Azure SDK can be useful tools when it comes time to develop a new Azure resource and write code for it. From there, you may choose the relevant option, such creating an Azure Mobile Service or a new Azure Cloud Service, among others.

275

Jason Taylor

QuickStarts section includes sample projects for particular
Azure technologies that Microsoft has made available. This

276

can be an excellent method for learning the fundamentals of a new or unknown technology.

277

CHAPTER TEN

POWERSHELL FOR WINDOWS

One of the most effective tools for developing and overseeing Azure-hosted solutions is Visual Studio. Despite its greatness, Visual Studio may not be the best tool for every situation. A scriptable tool like PowerShell would be a better option instead.

The following are some situations when PowerShell would be better:

- A resource for IT specialists Visual Studio is not often used by IT professionals to manage on-premises assets. Additionally, it makes reasonable that they wouldn't want to utilize Visual Studio for materials housed on Azure. Rather, PowerShell is frequently used, particularly when it comes to Windows environment management.

- Automating Azure resource deployment and provisioning Azure resource deployment and provisioning may be automated with PowerShell's robust scripting environment.

- Automating the provisioning of new Azure virtual machines, creating Azure Storage accounts, creating Azure websites, creating and importing Azure

278

Virtual Network settings, deploying Cloud Services, and much more can all be done with PowerShell scripts.

- Another excellent technique to lower the possibility of errors is to automate routine processes in Azure using PowerShell scripts. With the assurance that the same outcomes will always be obtained, the scripts can be extensively tested, protected in a source control system, and used frequently.

- It is advantageous to automate an activity that you will be performing on a regular basis. Developing the script may need more effort at first, but it will save a significant amount of time each time it is used. Using new or sophisticated Azure features that aren't available through the administration portal or Azure tools for Visual Studio Features that are not yet accessible in Visual Studio, such as establishing nondefault configuration options for the Azure load balancer or advance IP configuration for Azure virtual machines, are included in the Azure PowerShell cmdlets.

Compared to the Azure SDK for Visual Studio, the Azure PowerShell cmdlets are updated and released more frequently. As a result, new features frequently show up in

279

the PowerShell cmdlets (and REST API) before they do in Visual Studio. Furthermore, new features are frequently published that appear in the Azure PowerShell cmdlets but are initially not visible in either of the management portals. Before releasing the functionality to the management portals and any associated user interface components, the Microsoft Azure product team can release the feature and, in certain situations, refine it. The new Azure Files feature is a perfect illustration of this.

HOW TO INSTALL AZURE POWERSHELL CMDLET

You can download the stand-alone installer from GitHub or use the Web Platform Installer (Web PI) to get the Azure PowerShell cmdlets. The Azure PowerShell cmdlets can be installed by starting Web PI from this same location. Depending on the Azure SDK version you are using for your ongoing projects, installing the Azure PowerShell cmdlets via Web PI may also install the most recent version of the Azure SDK, which may or may not be desirable. Get the standalone installer from GitHub if you only want the Azure PowerShell cmdlets.

- To install the Azure PowerShell cmdlets, click the Windows Standalone link in the GitHub repository to obtain a normal Windows MSI.

Advice On the Azure PowerShell GitHub page, make sure to read the comprehensive documentation. In addition to many functionalities, the page offers a plethora of information on how to get started with the Azure cmdlets.

HOW TO ESTABLISH A CONNECTION WITH AZURE

You need to have an Azure subscription in order to connect to Azure. You must have a Microsoft account or a work or school (previously organizational) account in order to register for a free trial:

(at http://azure(dot)microsoft(dot)com).

You will link PowerShell to your Microsoft Azure subscription or subscriptions after installing the Azure PowerShell cmdlets. Using a management certificate or a Microsoft account are the two ways to connect to, or authenticate, with Microsoft Azure.

281

HOW TO USE A MICROSOFT ACCOUNT TO CONNECT

To access your Microsoft Azure subscription(s), you can use your Microsoft account (hotmail.com, outlook.com, etc.) or a work or school account (formerly an organization account; contoso.com, for example). Azure Active Directory (Azure AD) is used for this connection technique. Because it is simpler to control access to a subscription (particularly for a shared subscription that many users use), this is frequently the recommended approach. Additionally, to deal with the Azure Resource Manager API, the Azure AD technique must be used.

Use these procedures to establish a connection to your Microsoft Azure subscription:

- Launch the PowerShell console for Microsoft Azure. You may locate PowerShell on a Windows 8 computer by using the integrated Search function. Choose the Microsoft Azure PowerShell option to launch the console.
- Type the command Add-AzureAccount.
- You are prompted for your password and email address in a dialog window. Azure AD is used to

282

authenticate your credentials, and your roaming user profile contains your subscription information.

283

- Additionally, an access token that gives PowerShell access to your Azure resources is obtained. You will need to reauthenticate using Add-AzureAccount after this token expires because it is not permanent.

```
$userName = "<your work or school account user name>"

$securePassword = ConvertTo-SecureString -String "<your work or school account password>" -AsPlainText -Force

$cred = New-Object System.Management.Automation.PSCredential($userName, $securePassword) Add-AzureAccount -Credential $cred
```

284

Use the Get-AzureSubscription cmdlet to see every subscription that is available. Use the Select-AzureSubscription cmdlet to switch to a different subscription. The pop-up window should be avoided if you are using PowerShell for an automation script. In this instance, as demonstrated in the sample below, supply your credentials using the Credential argument. Only accounts used for work or school are compatible with the Credential option.

HOW TO USE A MANAGEMENT CERTIFICATE TO CONNECT

If you do not wish to use the Azure AD solution previously discussed, you can connect to your Azure subscription(s) using a management certificate. An X.509 v3 certificate that authenticates a client application (such PowerShell, Visual Studio, or custom code) is called an Azure management certificate and so forth) that makes use of the Azure Service Management API. Allowing the Azure Management Portal to create a management certificate for you is the simplest method.

- Launch the console for Azure PowerShell.
- Type the command Get-AzurePublishSettingsFile. This will download a.publishsettings file

285

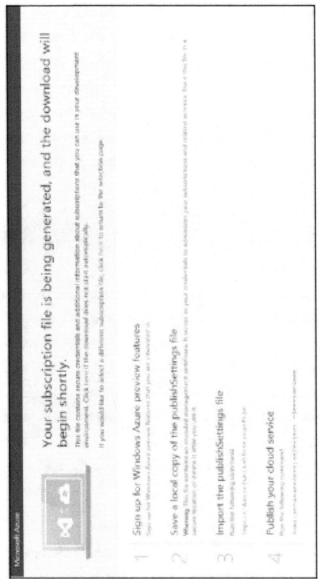

automatically and open a page on the Azure

286

Management Portal. You must use your administrative login information to access the Azure Management Portal. Your Microsoft Azure subscription(s) and any required management certificates are listed in the.publishsettings file.

- Locally save the.publishsettings file. Because it includes the management certificate and subscription information, please do not make this file publicly available. Any action against the subscription(s) can be taken by anyone with access to this file.

- Use the Import-AzurePublishSettingsFile to import the.publishsettings file.

ADVICE: The subscription ID and management certificate, among other private data pertaining to your Microsoft Azure subscriptions, are contained in the.publishsettings file. The file shouldn't be accessed by unauthorized individuals. After importing, it is advised that you remove the file.

A management certificate can be produced and configured to be used by PowerShell as an alternative. As an administrator, launch a Visual Studio command prompt and type the following command:

287

```
makecert -sky exchange -r -n "CN=<CertificateName>" -pe -a sha1 -len 2048 -ss My
"<CertificateName>.cer"
```

ADVICE: In Windows 8, search for "Visual Studio tools" to locate the Visual Studio command prompt. Developer Command Prompt is one of the shortcuts for Visual Studio

288

tools that may be used by opening the shortcut folder, which opens a Windows Explorer directory. Run As Administrator can be chosen by right-clicking the shortcut.

- Use the Azure Management Portal to upload the management certificate to Azure. Click MANAGEMENT CERTIFICATES on the Settings screen, and then select UPLOAD from the command bar at the bottom.
- Launch the PowerShell console for Microsoft Azure.

POWERSHELL MODES FOR AZURE

The Azure Resource Manager API and the Azure Service Management API are the two management APIs available in Azure. The first management API was the Azure Service Management API. The Azure Service Management API is used to programmatically interface with Azure by a number of current programs, including Visual Studio, PowerShell, the Azure Management Portal, and other third-party applications. One new management API is the Azure Resource Manager API, which is still in Preview as of this writing. Azure Resource Manager enables you to organize resources according to the solution you wish to develop, such as a blog, an e-commerce site, a data processing service, and so on, rather than working with individual

289

resources (storage account, virtual machine, Azure SQL database, etc.). The materials required to belong to a resource group and collectively make up the solution.

The ability to switch between these two management APIs is part of the Azure PowerShell installation. There are two PowerShell modules installed: AzureResourceManager, which connects to the Azure Resource Manager API, and Azure, which connects to the Service Management API. When you launch the Azure PowerShell console, the Azure module is automatically imported into the active session. The transition-AzureMode cmdlet is used to transition between modules. For instance, use the convert-AzureMode AzureResourceManager cmdlet to convert to utilizing Azure Resource Manager. Use the Switch-AzureMode AzureServiceManagement cmdlet to return to the Azure Service Management API.

To work with the different Azure resources, there are numerous cmdlets available. Enter the command get-help azure to obtain a list of all the cmdlets. The following example demonstrates how the Azure PowerShell cmdlets can streamline the common task of creating a new Azure virtual machine.

290

Advice The PowerShell variable $DebugPreference = "Continue" is set in the example above. When attempting to determine why a command could fail or not function as intended, doing so can be helpful. When "Continue" is selected for $DebugPreference, the console will display the underlying REST API request and response.

INTERFACE FOR CROSS-PLATFORM COMMAND-LINE

The PowerShell cmdlets, covered in the previous section, are the greatest choice for Windows users who want to operate from the command line and automate processes, particularly when scripting the provisioning of many Azure resources. On the other hand, the Azure Cross-Platform Command-Line Interface (sometimes called xplat-cli) offers a consistent experience for Windows, Mac OS, and Linux users in mixed situations.

The xplat-cli repository is accessible on GitHub at https://github(dot)com/Azure/azure-xplat-cli, just as the Azure PowerShell project repository.

SETTING UP

The Azure SDK for Node.js was used to create the Node.js application known as xplat-cli. As a result, make sure Node.js is installed on your computer.

291

SETTING UP ON WINDOWS

292

If you don't already have Node.js installed on your computer. Web PI will install the xplat-cli and Node.js. Installing Node.js via the http://nodejs(dot)org website is an alternative.

To start the process of installing the most recent version, simply click INSTALL. You can install the xplat-cli using npm (Node Package Manager) after installing Node.js on your computer.

npm install azure-cli -g

NPM will set up all required dependencies.

After the installation is complete, type Azure into the command prompt to start the xplat-cli. You will now see "AZURE" in ASCII art, the version number, and some rudimentary help information when the xplat-cli launches (albeit it may take a few seconds).

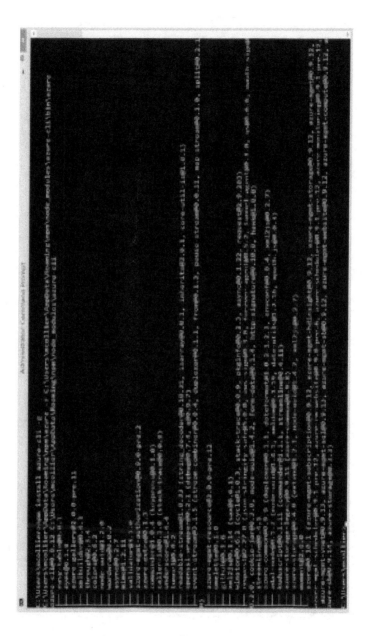

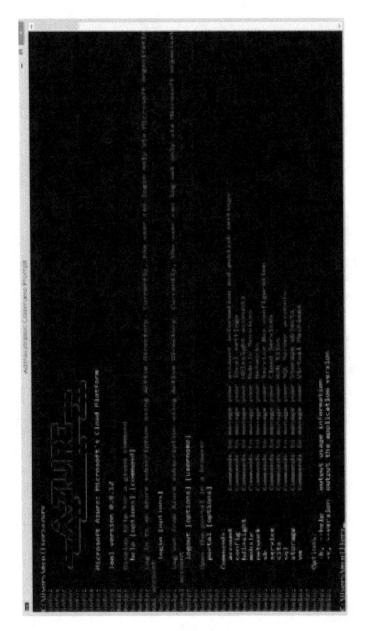

296

SETTING UP ON LINUX

The xplat-cli can be installed on Linux systems in a manner that is functionally identical to that of Windows systems. You must make sure that Node.js is installed. The package management that corresponds to your Linux distribution can be used. For instance, run the following command on CentOS:

sudo   curl   -sL   Setup | bash: https://rpm.nodesource.com/setup

Next,   run   the   subsequent   command:

```
sudo yum install -y nodejs
```

Once you're done, run the Azure command. This will produce the same outcomes as running the command on a Windows system.

ESTABLISHING A CONNECTION WITH AZURE

You must first establish a connection to your Microsoft Azure subscription or subscriptions before you can start using the xplat-cli. The options for using the Azure PowerShell cmdlets and the xplat-cli are fairly similar. Using a management certificate or a work or school account are the two choices.

Jason Taylor

HOW TO USE A MANAGEMENT CERTIFICATE TO CONNECT

The simplest way to obtain a management certificate is to let the Azure Management Portal to generate one, which is similar to using the Azure PowerShell cmdlets. A.publishsettings file is the format in which the management certificate is delivered.

- Use the following command to get a.publishsettings file if you don't already have one. You will be prompted to sign in when the Azure Management Portal opens.

```
azure account download
```

- After modifying to use the location of the file on your machine, import the.publishsettings file by running the following command:

```
Azure account import [path to your .publishsettings file]
```

ADVICE: The subscription ID and management certificate, among other private data pertaining to your Microsoft Azure subscriptions, are contained in the.publishsettings file. The file shouldn't be accessed by unauthorized individuals. After importing, it is advised that you remove the file. Use a work or school account to connect.

As an alternative, you can connect to your Microsoft Azure subscription or subscriptions using an Azure AD account from work or school (previously an organizational account).

- To log in with a work or school account, use the following command:

azure login -u username -p password

- As an alternative, you can log in interactively by running the Azure login command without entering your username or password. This stops credentials from appearing in plain text on the screen.

TAKE NOTE: Using a Microsoft account will not work with this strategy. You must establish a new user in your default Azure AD directory and designate the user as a co-administrator for your Azure subscription if you are managing your Azure subscription(s) with a Microsoft account.

USE

The syntax for using the xplat-cli is simple: azure account list or azure vm start web-fe-1 are examples of —azure [subject] [verb] [options]. You may view the top-level list of

299

topics (account, vm, service, etc.) by simply using the Azure command. All you have to do is type in Azure and the topic you want to learn more about. For instance, Azure Virtual Machine will provide the instructions that can be used to operate with Azure Virtual Machines.

With the xplat-cli, you can accomplish a lot of tasks. After it's finished, you ought to see a result which shows that the virtual machine was constructed.

CASES FOR BUSINESSES

Microsoft Azure can be used for a variety of commercial purposes, such as creating temporary development and testing environments, expanding your on-premises infrastructure into the cloud, or creating new apps that utilize Azure's features. To help you come up with some ideas for using Azure, we go over a few typical scenarios in this chapter.

SCENARIOS FOR DEVELOPMENT AND TESTING

The development and testing (dev/test) workload is one of the most prevalent in Azure. Whether your production infrastructure is on-premises or currently operating in Azure, you can often replicate all or a portion of it there and utilize the replica for testing, development, or staging. Setting up a development/test environment in an on-

300

premises datacenter requires a number of tasks, including networking setup, firewall configuration, OS and other software installation, hardware acquisition, and more. This may require a significant length of time. After testing is complete, you must either repurpose the hardware or leave it idle until you need it again for testing. Azure allows you to provision the necessary resources (VMs, cloud services, websites, storage, etc.) and start testing in a matter of minutes. You can terminate all of the services and cease paying for them after the testing is complete. The deployment and deconstruction of your development/test environment may really be scripted with Azure.

The best part is that you can quickly scale your dev/test environment to meet your current needs as your infrastructure expands. It is necessary to repeat the acquisition and configuration process when using on-premises dev/test infrastructure.

You can still use Azure for development and testing if everything is on-premises. Your on-premises network can be extended into Azure by setting up a virtual network. You could have a web application operating in your local datacenter that connects to SQL Server hosted in Azure, for instance, and you might wish to test your application against a new version of SQL Server.

You receive a monthly credit to spend for your Azure development and testing infrastructure if you have an MSDN subscription. Additionally, there are discounts available for a number of the services. VMs, for instance, have a 33% discount. The total cost of establishing and utilizing a dev/test infrastructure might be greatly reduced as a result. You can use Azure to rapidly replicate the components of your infrastructure in the following additional business cases.

You may experiment quickly with minor things. For example, let's imagine you want to test only one thing. For instance, you may wish to alter how something appears on your website, but you are unsure of its feasibility or functionality. With the settings pointing to the production backend, you can deploy the updated website as a new one after making the necessary changes. After that, you can evaluate the visual layout and process and determine whether it makes sense to build up a full development/test environment.

You can perform load testing on a complete clone of your production environment after creating it. This can include

302

virtual networks, storage, webpages, VMs, various cloud services, and so on. In addition to allowing you to do load testing without interfering with any production services, this can assist you in identifying possible process bottlenecks so you can address them before they have an impact on your customers.

To determine the extent of the resources required to manage various loads, such as the size of the virtual machines or the quantity of cloud service instances, load testing can be employed. If possible, you can then configure the computing services to do autoscaling. For instance, you may find that your website becomes unusable when the CPU utilization percentage rises above 60%. In this case, you may choose to use autoscaling to raise the number of instances when the CPU utilization reaches the desired level. Load testing improves your customer's experience in general.

Software upgrades Before upgrading your production services, you should check for compatibility between your software and the software of the company you are utilizing if you are using software from an outside source. To make your product compatible with the latest version of SQL Server, you may need to make changes and go through the

303

entire testing, staging, and implementation process. You can most likely obtain a prerelease copy or a complimentary short-term trial of the updated version in an on-premises setting. But in order to execute it, you need infrastructure, thus just like in the earlier examples, you may need to buy hardware and other things. As with Windows, SQL Server, Oracle, and Linux, among other programs, the software may be offered as a preconfigured virtual machine (VM) on Azure. Then, in a dev/test environment, you can simply provision a new virtual machine (VM) with the updated version and execute your app against it. You can provision a Windows or Linux virtual machine (VM), install the updated software, and utilize it for your development and testing scenario if Azure does not provide any predefined virtual machines.

A/B testing Assume you wish to conduct some A/B testing on your website without having to repeatedly deploy the various iterations. Multiple deployment slots are supported by Azure Websites. Versions A and B can be published to different slots and then switched them in and out of production as necessary to conduct the metrics collecting and testing.

Using Azure Traffic Manager's weighted round-robin load balancing is an additional choice. With Traffic Manager, you may use round robin, failover, and performance load balancing techniques to distribute incoming traffic among several services. Round-robin load balancing allows you to assign weights to the various deployments. This implies that in order to conduct A/B testing, you can redirect a tiny portion of traffic to a different deployment.

SITUATIONS THAT ARE HYBRID

The number of businesses using cloud-based solutions is growing at an astounding rate. Other organizations are inspired to follow suit by their success. Due to legal concerns or the inability of certain workloads to function in a virtualized environment, some organizations will not be able to migrate all of their workloads to the cloud. on these situations, hybrid computing—where a business operates some of its infrastructure on-site and some on the cloud—will be a crucial tactic.

One excellent example of hybrid computing is the Microsoft Azure platform. An on-premises datacenter can be connected to one or more Azure regions in a variety of ways. Azure offers both site-to-site and point-to-site virtual network connectivity, as covered in Chapter 5, Azure Virtual

Networks. A secure VPN connection between Azure-hosted resources and on-premises assets is offered by both options. Azure ExpressRoute is an extra hybrid connectivity option that allows a private connection between Azure and your colocation facility or on-premises equipment without using the public Internet.

CHAPTER ELEVEN
CONNECTIVITY TO THE NETWORK

Hybrid connectivity is a crucial scenario for the Azure platform, regardless of the solution selected—site-to-site, point-to-site, or ExpressRoute. There are numerous opportunities to expand an on-premises infrastructure to the cloud by establishing a hybrid link. The following are two typical situations for network-enabled hybrid connectivity: Keeping the database on-premises while hosting a website in Azure One of the more challenging tasks in an organization's cloud migration process is moving on-premises data to Azure. Typically, the challenge manifests as either a technological problem or a demand for compliance. Technically speaking, for instance, the application in question is made to use a database that Azure does not support. Regarding compliance, it's possible that Azure SQL Database or database operation cannot satisfy a regulatory obligation.

(MongoDB, SQL Server, etc.) on Azure virtual machines. In these situations, a company may decide to use Azure Websites or Azure Cloud Services (via a web role) to host the website in Azure while keeping the database on-site. One of the previously described technologies might then be used to create connectivity between the website and the database:

307

a ExpressRoute, a point-to-site connection, or a site-to-site link.

HOW TO USE AN ON-PREMISES SERVICE

Occasionally, a website is dependent on a specific service that isn't transferable to the cloud. Maybe the website relies on an API to do a critical business calculation, and that API cannot be relocated due to security concerns, the fact that other on-premises services rely on the service, or the fact that it is legacy technology that Azure does not support. To enable the Azure-hosted website to easily communicate with the required API that still exists on-premises, a hybrid connection is created between Azure and the on-premises architecture. In this case, accessing an on-premises service could be done via an Azure Service Bus Relay in addition to a network connection.

INTERNET ACCESS

In many situations, a simple Internet connection is sufficient instead of a specialized hybrid connectivity solution. After all, one of the alluring aspects of cloud computing is its capacity to connect to services that are accessible over the Internet. Typical situations include the following: Archival data storage It can be very costly to keep large volumes of data on-site, particularly archival material that is rarely accessed. Infrastructure, personnel, software licenses, and physical space costs can quickly place a heavy financial strain on a company. As covered in Chapter 4, Azure Storage, Azure offers almost infinite storage space at a remarkably low cost. A company may want to use Azure Blob storage's scalable storage as a place to archive data. When the data is required, the on-premises service or services download it from Azure Blob storage and process it as needed. Although an ExpressRoute connection could be used for increased speed and security, a regular Internet connection will usually be adequate.

Microsoft Azure StorSimple provides an additional choice for archival data storage. One of the hardware appliances that comes with StorSimple is installed on-site. Data that is often accessed is stored locally by the appliance. Data automatically moves to Azure Blob storage when it ages (is accessed less frequently). Organizations have the option to synchronize their Azure AD users and groups with user and group information from their Active Directory on-site.

In doing so, users can choose to use Azure Active Directory Sync (AADSync; previously known as DirSync) to synchronize the user data and a password hash, making Azure AD the authority for user authentication.

309

Alternatively, an organization might wish to synchronize the user data but require users to authenticate via an Active Directory Federation Services (AD FS) endpoint residing on premises, effectively redirecting the user to an on-premises AD FS site for authentication before redirecting to the desired location.

Occasionally, an organization's on-premises infrastructure cannot support the necessary load, so it bursts to the cloud. Perhaps there is a rush over the holidays or a time frame set by the government for enrolling in a crucial service. An company may decide to use the elastic nature of the cloud to scale back to simply on-premises services when the load returns to normal, rather than constructing the on-premises infrastructure to accommodate the brief spike in demand. In this case, a company may host the service on Azure Websites, Cloud Services, or Azure Virtual Machines and employ autoscale rules to make sure capacity meets customer demand.

HOW TO MODERNIZE AND TRANSFER OF APPLICATIONS AND INFRASTRUCTURE

Every application has to be upgraded at some point in its life. It can be a hardware update or a change of the user interface. The Azure platform can update the supporting infrastructure,

310

but it cannot assist in developing a visually appealing, contemporary user experience. Hardware refresh cycles are common in many organizations and usually occur roughly every three years. Organizations today face a new dilemma when it comes to hardware upgrades: should we use our infrastructure and services in the cloud or purchase new on-premises hardware?

In addition to the necessary hardware upgrade, an organization may decide to move to the cloud if its current on-premises datacenter has hit physical capacity constraints or will soon. It's possible that the existing datacenter lacks the physical capacity to accommodate additional servers or is unable to provide the required cooling or power. Perhaps there is a desire to decrease or do away with hardware infrastructure management in the future. The company may be able to exit the datacenter industry entirely or at least in part by moving to the cloud (see the section

Microsoft handles the datacenter's hardware and associated infrastructure, allowing the company to concentrate on offering excellent business solutions. Some businesses will decide to move to the cloud in order to gain capacity in new regions that they are unable to serve at the moment due to their lack of presence there or because it would be prohibitively expensive. Azure datacenters are located in 19 different regions worldwide, including two in China that are run and marketed by 21Vianet. Rather than establishing and sustaining a global datacenter presence, a company may choose to leverage Microsoft's current assets and implement to several areas effortlessly. There are undoubtedly many Azure resources available if the decision is made to update or move to the cloud. An organization may have a number of questions when deciding to use these resources, such as the following:

- Should we use IaaS, PaaS, or both?
- Should we use platform-provided services like Azure
- Search or Azure Media Services rather than keeping up a proprietary solution?
- Should we relocate all of the parts or just some of them?
- For our needs, which hybrid model is best?
- Which Azure region or regions ought to be utilized?
- What impact does Azure use have on our operations and business model?
- What is our SLA?
- What is our disaster recovery story?

312

MOBILE SERVICES ON AZURE

You can find mobile devices everywhere these days, including tablets, phones, watches, and fitness bands. A business can benefit greatly from having a mobile application, whether it is utilized internally, externally, or both.

Microsoft Azure Mobile Services is a Backend-as-a-Service that offers a number of features to facilitate the development of mobile applications more quickly and easily. Because mobile services are adaptable and scalable, you may scale your application to meet the demands of your users as it gains popularity.

The fact that you only need to create one backend version is another benefit of using Azure Mobile Services. You can reach every customer on any platform without putting in extra effort because the backend is compatible with iOS, Android, and Windows devices.

Azure Mobile Services offers a number of features, including the following. Although it is possible to develop a service to incorporate these functionalities from scratch, Azure Mobile Services saves you the time and expense required to do so.

313

Storage of data You can decide to use SQL Database to power your data storage because it provides an easy-to-use interface that doesn't require a DBA. Additionally, SQL Server, Oracle, SAP, MongoDB, and Azure Table storage can all be integrated. When your program is ready to go online again, you can write it to function offline and synchronize the data. Because the work will be saved on the backend when connectivity is restored, the customer can continue working even if they are unable to access the Internet.

Data authorization and user authentication are significantly streamlined. SSO is simple to set up with Google, Facebook, Twitter, Microsoft, and Azure AD. Push alerts Using Microsoft Azure Notification Hubs, you can convey information about enterprise and customer apps to any customer's mobile device. Any backend, whether on-site or hosted in Azure, can provide this. The server-side code needed to send messages to the push notification services for iOS, Android, and Windows Phone devices is automatically handled by Notification Hubs.

Targeting audiences by activity, interest, location, or choice is possible using Notification Hubs' tagging capability. Additionally, you may deliver localized push notifications in

314

the customer's native tongue using Notification Hubs' templates feature.

Because Azure powers Mobile Services, scaling in and out to satisfy client demand is simple. You may even configure autoscaling to manage millions of devices by scaling out automatically as demand rises. Backend processing on the server can be scheduled using Microsoft Azure Scheduler. For instance, you may want to set up a scheduled job that asks your on-premises database for an update and saves the updated data in a table so your mobile application can receive it later. It is possible to establish a hybrid connection. The mobile application can be linked to SharePoint, Office 365, and on-premises applications using this connection.

315

CONCLUSION

As we draw to a close on our extensive exploration of Microsoft Azure, it's crucial to take a moment to reflect on the substantial journey we have undertaken together. This tutorial has aimed not just to impart knowledge but to equip you with the skills and confidence necessary to navigate the vast and dynamic landscape of cloud computing. In a world where technology is advancing at breakneck speed, mastering Azure is not merely a professional asset; it is a necessity for those looking to thrive in the digital era.

RECAP OF KEY LEARNINGS

Throughout this book, we have traversed a wide array of topics, starting with the foundational principles of cloud computing and ascending to more complex scenarios involving Azure's rich set of services. We began with an overview of Azure's architecture and the core components that form its backbone: Azure Compute, Azure Storage, and Azure Networking. Each of these services is integral to the development and deployment of applications in the cloud, providing developers with the necessary tools to create scalable, resilient, and efficient solutions.

In our discussions on Azure's Infrastructure as a Service (IaaS), Platform as a Service (PaaS), and Software as a Service (SaaS) models, we highlighted how these frameworks cater to different business needs. The practical exercises provided throughout the book were designed to give you hands-on experience, allowing you to apply theoretical concepts in real-world scenarios. This experiential learning is vital in solidifying your understanding and preparing you for the challenges you may face in your career.

We also explored Azure's governance and management features, which are crucial for maintaining oversight and control over your cloud environment. Tools such as Azure Policy, Azure Resource Manager, and Azure Blueprints play significant roles in ensuring compliance with organizational standards and best practices. Understanding how to leverage these tools will help you maintain a well-organized and efficient cloud infrastructure.

Security and Compliance: A Fundamental Focus

In an era where data breaches and cyber threats are alarmingly prevalent, we dedicated significant attention to security and compliance. Azure offers a robust suite of security features designed to protect your applications and

317

317

data. We examined tools like Azure Security Center and Azure Sentinel, which provide comprehensive insights into your security posture and help to mitigate risks through proactive monitoring and threat detection.

Compliance is another critical aspect of cloud computing. Organizations are increasingly concerned about the regulatory landscape, and Azure's adherence to various compliance standards gives users peace of mind. We discussed how Azure facilitates compliance with regulations such as GDPR, HIPAA, and others, allowing you to build trust with your clients and stakeholders.

The Importance of Continuous Learning

A key takeaway from this tutorial is the necessity of adopting a mindset of continuous learning. The cloud computing landscape, particularly Azure, is in a constant state of flux. Microsoft regularly updates its offerings and introduces new features that enhance the platform's functionality and performance. Staying informed about these changes is essential for maximizing the benefits of Azure.

Engaging with the Azure community—through forums, webinars, and user groups—can provide you with a wealth of information that extends beyond the material covered in this book. The collaborative spirit of the tech community is

318

a powerful resource, offering insights into best practices, innovative solutions, and real-world experiences that can enhance your understanding of Azure and its applications.

Real-World Applications and Future Trends

As you contemplate your next steps, consider how the skills and knowledge you've gained can be applied to your projects and career aspirations. The ability to design, implement, and manage applications in the cloud is increasingly sought after across various industries. Mastering Azure can open doors to opportunities in software development, data analytics, cybersecurity, and beyond.

Looking towards the future, the trends in cloud computing are promising and dynamic. Technologies such as artificial intelligence (AI), machine learning (ML), and the Internet of Things (IoT) are reshaping how we interact with data and applications. Azure is at the forefront of these advancements, offering a suite of tools and services that facilitate the seamless integration of these cutting-edge technologies into your applications. By embracing these innovations, you can not only meet current demands but also anticipate future needs, positioning yourself as a forward-thinking professional.

319

The Role of Azure in Digital Transformation

As organizations increasingly undergo digital transformation, Azure plays a pivotal role in this journey. Businesses are leveraging cloud capabilities to enhance their agility, streamline operations, and foster innovation. Understanding how to effectively navigate Azure's offerings positions you as a valuable asset to any organization looking to thrive in the digital age.

Digital transformation is not just about technology; it is also about culture and strategy. Companies that adopt a cloud-first approach are often more adaptable to market changes, better equipped to respond to customer needs, and more innovative in their product offerings. By mastering Azure, you become a key player in this transformation, enabling organizations to leverage the cloud for competitive advantage.

Building a Network and Collaborating

One of the most valuable aspects of your journey through Azure is the opportunity to build a network with fellow learners and professionals. Collaborating with others can lead to new ideas, perspectives, and even career opportunities. Consider participating in local meetups, online forums, or even contributing to open-source projects.

320

These activities not only enhance your learning experience but also allow you to connect with like-minded individuals who share your passion for cloud computing.

Final Thoughts

In conclusion, mastering Microsoft Azure is more than just acquiring technical skills; it is a strategic investment in your professional toolkit. The knowledge and competencies you have developed throughout this tutorial will serve as a solid foundation for building and scaling applications in the cloud.

As you move forward, remember that the journey does not end here; it is merely the beginning. The cloud landscape is vast and full of opportunities for those willing to explore and innovate. Continue to engage with Azure's resources, experiment with new features, and seek out community-driven knowledge. This proactive approach will empower you to stay ahead in a rapidly changing technological environment.

Thank you for joining me on this in-depth journey through Azure. I hope this book has equipped you not only with the technical skills necessary to succeed but also with the inspiration to innovate and push the boundaries of what is possible in the cloud. Embrace the future of technology with confidence and creativity, and you will undoubtedly make a significant impact in your field. The world of cloud computing awaits you—go forth and make your mark!

322

www.ingramcontent.com/pod-product-compliance
Lightning Source LLC
LaVergne TN
LVHW022335060326
832902LV00022B/4042

* 9 7 9 8 3 0 8 9 8 3 8 4 2 *